Spiritual
WARFARE

DR. JACK SCHAAP

Acknowledgement

I owe a great debt of gratitude to my editorial advisor, Mr. Matthew Sheehy, who has labored countless hours to make my thoughts and my heart clear to my readers. Matthew Sheehy was born in New York City. He graduated from the SUNY College of Environmental Science and Forestry at Syracuse University in 1997 with a B.S. in chemistry. He then attended Duke University in Durham, North Carolina, with the intention of earning a Ph.D. in chemistry. Upon being called to the ministry under the preaching of Dr. Rick Finley at Fellowship Baptist Church, he left Duke University with an M.S. degree and moved to Northwest Indiana. He began attending the First Baptist Church of Hammond, Indiana, and Hyles-Anderson College in 2000. Matthew graduated from Hyles-Anderson in 2003 with a master's degree in pastoral theology. For the past five years, he has served as a Bible teacher and as the academic advisor at Hammond Baptist High School. Matthew married his wife, Amy, on July 24, 1999. They now reside in Crown Point, Indiana.

Dedication

I dedicate this book to the generational warriors who have accepted the challenge and responsibility of pulling down the strongholds in their own lives and those of their loved ones.

May God grant you His grace to stand.

1st Printing – March 2009

ISBN: 978-0-9819603-0-2

All Scripture quotations are from the King James Bible.

Project Manager: Dr. Bob Marshall
Assistant: Rochelle Chalifoux
Transcription: Cyndilu Marshall
Cover Design: Jon Suh and Doug Wruck
Page Design and Layout: Kristi Wertz
Proofreading: Debbie Borsh, Kelly Cervantes, Rena Fish

To order additional books by Dr. Jack Schaap,
please contact:
Hyles Publications
523 Sibley Street
Hammond, Indiana 46320
www.hylespublications.com
e-mail: info@hylespublications.com

Spiritual WARFARE

Dr. Jack Schaap

About the Author

Dr. Jack Schaap is the senior pastor of First Baptist Church of Hammond, Indiana, recognized as one of the largest congregations in America. He has a B.S., an M.Ed., and a D.D. from Hyles-Anderson College in Crown Point, Indiana.

Dr. Schaap counsels approximately 100 church members weekly; he superintends more than 3,000 Christian young people in five separate church-operated, private Christian schools, including one in China. Dr. Schaap is the chancellor of Hyles-Anderson College, a private Bible college which First Baptist Church operates for the purpose of training preachers, missionaries, and Christian educators. For more than 20 years, he preached 35 yearly meetings to tens of thousands of teenagers. First Baptist Church has the largest children's and teens' ministries in America. Dr. Schaap is the author of 17 books and several pamphlets.

Dr. Schaap has been married to his wife Cindy since 1979, and they have two adult children who serve in the ministries of First Baptist Church.

Table of Contents

Section Three – The Battleground

Section Four – The Battle Plan

Introduction

Spiritual warfare. The words conjure up images of ghastly demons battling glowing angels and Satan prowling the earth seeking whom he may devour. Perhaps spiritual warfare reminds most people of white witches, black witches, black magic, and white magic. Spiritual warfare might invoke images of animal sacrifice and drinking blood. Maybe it summons thoughts of Ouija boards, casting spells, and playing rock music backwards.

And Satan is thrilled if spiritual warfare is dismissed as the occult.

Satan has used a lot of smoke and mirrors to distract Christians from the real matter of spiritual warfare. His battle waged against their spirit concerns their relationships. His battle is against a Christian's thoughts and words. His battle is against the generations to come. He hopes to destroy them by destroying this generation.

The destruction that Satan brings isn't bloody and gruesome. It is a festering process that probes and exploits a Christian's weaknesses. His attacks deflate their spirit and leaves them spiritually paralyzed.

Satan doesn't want Christians to hold séances and offer animal sacrifices. He wants them to run their mouths and ruin their minds. He wants to instill a poor spirit in them so that they can contaminate others.

Many Christians temporarily soothe the pains of life through complaints and strife. They have lost the divine perspective. They resort to worldly logic and carnal distractions to deliver themselves from their struggles. Jesus said that we would enter Heaven through much tribulation. The journey is rough, and few Christians have prepared themselves with the right tools and the right perspective for the long run.

Losers in spiritual warfare are choosing misery, divorce, strife, contention, anger, frustration, depression, hatred, and wrath.

Why are Christians so victimized by the world when there is great hope for the believer?

Why are they so unsuccessful in reaching the next generation when they have such a tremendous arsenal of weapons to defeat every vice against them?

Why do they choose the discouragement of living the defeated Christian life?

Christians don't have to!

The first step is to understand the enemy and the battle he wages against you. The second step is to accept the challenge of being a warrior. The third step is to learn and use the spiritual weapons that God provides. The last step is to ensure that it all leads you to a better relationship with God.

This book is for those who seek the victorious Christian life. This book is for the Christian who looks at the generations of repetitive sin in his family and says, "It doesn't have to be this way." *Spiritual Warfare* is for the Christian who feels that God is calling him out of the average Christian life for His glorification. This book is for the one who feels life or Satan or God has thrashed him and says, "What can I do from here?"

Spiritual Warfare is a simple attempt to help those who are responsible for the next generation. It is for moms and dads, grandparents, teachers, bus workers, and anyone else who wants to give the next generation the opportunity to excel for the sake of Christ.

Section One

THE BACKGROUND

Chapter One

The Essence of Spiritual Warfare

Water is the medium in which fish swim. Musical notes comprise an orchestral piece. Air is the medium in which sound travels. In a similar way, words are the medium of spiritual warfare. Words comprise the thoughts that divide us from our God-ordained relationships.

Jesus said in John 6:63, *"It is the spirit that quickeneth; the flesh profiteth nothing: the words that I speak unto you, they are spirit, and they are life."* Words are spirit. My spirit is what I think in words and what I say in words. Spiritual warfare is a battle over the words and thoughts that provoke us to actions.

The Apostle John said in I John 4:1-2, *"Beloved, believe not every spirit, but try the spirits whether they are of God: because many false prophets are gone out into the world. Hereby know ye the Spirit of God: Every spirit that confesseth that Jesus Christ is come in the flesh is of God."* Verses 3 and 5 of the same chapter also state that spirits confess or speak. Since speaking is done with the mouth and confession is often made with the mouth, we can conclude that spirits have everything to do with words.

An Example From Marriage

A husband and wife visited me for a counseling appointment. The man repetitively said unkind things about his wife.

The wife said that he always made these horrible statements. She then made unkind remarks about him.

The husband responded with the same barbs and accusations he had previously spouted.

I said, "Stop a minute. Why don't you tell me what you really believe about your wife?"

He said, "I am."

"No, you're not. You are telling me what you have formed a habit of saying. Tell me what you believe in your heart about your wife."

Instead of telling me, he turned his chair toward his wife. "I am going to tell you what I think about you." I was worried that the situation would explode.

Before the next words came from his mouth, the spirit in the room changed. The angry spirit subsided. The husband said, "I think you are very beautiful. You are a great cook." He looked at me and said, "My wife is a great cook." He turned back to her and said, "You do a great job with the kids considering that I'm always gone to work."

Her eyes glistened with tears.

I asked her, "How are you feeling right now?"

She said, "I am feeling very loved. If I had heard these words in the last couple of weeks, we wouldn't be in your office right now. I feel very accepted by the man who loves me."

He reached over and grabbed his wife's hands. He asked me, "Could you give us a few minutes alone?"

I left the two of them in my office. Fifteen minutes later I knocked on my office door and entered. The spirit was very warm because this husband had spoken words from his heart.

Words Create a Spirit.

You create a negative or positive spirit by the words you think or say. Spiritual warfare is not a physical fight. Spiritual warfare is a fight taking place in your mind, heart, and body. It is fought through your thoughts and feelings.

Have you ever walked into a hostile atmosphere and thought that there was a bad spirit in the room? The bad spirit was not ghosts flying around. The bad spirit was created by the negative thoughts and negative words toward you. Similarly, if you were in a room where people were supporting you, you would feel a positive spirit. As you listen to people speak, your spirit changes. Words help you determine whether or not you fit into a crowd.

Surely you have walked out of a church service and said, "I'm glad I came today. That really helped me." You were changed by the words of a song, a sermon, or a Christian brother. You won a spiritual battle because your thoughts and words were pleasant.

Your spirit is the words you really do believe and say. When the Bible says, "...*Every spirit that confesseth that Jesus Christ is come in the flesh is of God,*" it does not simply mean every spirit that says that Jesus Christ is come in the flesh is of God. Confession involves speaking the truth in your heart. You can say anything, but you have to believe it in your heart. The Bible teaches in Romans 10:9 that salvation is obtained when the belief of your heart (that Jesus paid for all of your sins) is expressed.

Spiritual warfare deals with the war in our hearts and our

minds to form our thoughts and words. Spiritual warfare is a word battle. People don't even have to verbalize those words to affect your spirit. You can feel them through their posture.

Words affect your posture. How many times has a wife told her husband, "Whatever you say!" with her arms folded? She really means that it is not okay. Your words can say one thing while your mind is filled with doubt, distrust, suspicion, and accusation.

Since your spirit is determined by the words you say and by the actions that confirm your words, spiritual warfare is a war of your mind and mouth. If you can control your mind and mouth, you win the battle.

Jesus Christ spoke what was in His heart. This is why He was called the Truth. Mark 2:8 says, *"And immediately when Jesus perceived in his spirit that they so reasoned within themselves, he said unto them, Why reason ye these things in your hearts?"* He said exactly what He meant, and His words were right on target.

How many times have you said what was not in your heart? That is called a lie. How many times have you presented an attitude that was not consistent with your spirit? How many times have you tried to be politically correct? Don't you find it refreshing when somebody speaks the truth that is in his heart?

Jesus listened to the Pharisees and perceived their spirit. He perceived that the words from their mouth were not the true intents of their heart. The Pharisees' spoken words were on God's side, but their thoughts were not. Jesus essentially asked them, "Why aren't your thoughts with Me? If you say you are with God, then how come you are not with Me?"

When your words and thoughts are in contradiction with the Bible, you give off a bad spirit. The bad spirit is a weapon in spiritual warfare. The words, thoughts, and postures interfere with your relationships. Satan loves it.

Spiritual warfare therefore is fought mainly within your mind and mouth. What you think and what you say determines your spiritual victories or defeats. Since you speak words, which you first think, the ultimate battle is in your mind. If you can learn the law of words, you can learn how to have spiritual victory.

The Greatest Damage in Spiritual Warfare Is Done by the Mouth.

Swords are great weapons in warfare, and the tongue might be the sharpest sword of all. Nothing divides our God-ordained relationships like a sharp tongue spewing acrid words toward another believer. We quickly blame Satan for our affliction, but much of it is encouraged by our fellow believers. The spiritual warfare is fought by two-faced, hypocritical Christians who are destroying God-ordained relationships.

Satan is described in I Peter 5 as an adversary and a devourer who gulps down a person. Satan is described in Revelation 12 as a deceiver and the accuser of the brethren. We are commanded to be sober and vigilant (alert and awake), guarding ourselves from his attacks. We are to be Satan's opponent, and James admonishes us to resist him steadfastly, refusing to budge an inch.

The book of Job details a conversation between God and Satan about a believer. Satan never acknowledged anything positive about Job. Satan accused Job, became his adversary, devoured Job, and deceived Job's wife and friends. As we look at Satan's dealings with God and Job, we should discover how much our mouth is like Satan's. We do his work for him.

Christians often become the adversary of other believers. They devour a person's character, testimony, and reputation. They accuse the brethren and deceive by misrepresenting to others what the person truly is in his character and actions. These Christians have their lives tuned in to Heaven while their mouths are wired to Hell.

Christians Act Like Satan When They Criticize Another Believer.

Satan said to God, "The only reason Job serves You is because of the blessings you give him." Satan was criticizing the motives and actions of Job and was ultimately criticizing the grace of God. Envy over material blessings will move many Christians to criticize others. Rich people judge poor people and write them off as lazy. Poor people criticize the rich and ignore that the rich person may have worked hard to get ahead in life. Critical questions are a critique of God's goodness to others.

When you criticize, you do the work of Satan. Christians also act like Satan when they sit in judgment over the reasons someone goes through a tough time. Job's friends did this. They told him that God took away his material goods because he wasn't very righteous.

James 2:1-4 teaches that when you respect people by what they wear (or their material blessing), you become *"judges of evil thoughts."* Your judgment of God is determined by the brand name on someone's clothes. Satanism is judging the material value of a person and deciding their value as a Christian based on their material value. This is why Satan claimed that if you stripped Job of his material blessings that he would be just like every other sorry Christian.

We tend to judge others in the actions that we perform ourselves. When you judge another man's Christianity, you are betraying the truth of your own weaknesses. Romans 2:1 says, *"Therefore thou art inexcusable, O man, whosoever thou art that judgest: for wherein thou judgest another, thou condemnest thyself; for thou that judgest doest the same things."*

Spiritual Warfare Creates a Spirit of Discouragement.

A person who is criticized will question his own values and worth and be depressed in his spirit. Job wasn't discouraged when he lost his children and his material possessions. Job 1:22 says, *"In all this Job sinned not, nor charged God foolishly."* He didn't struggle when he had boils on his body. Job said, *"What? shall we receive good at the hand of God, and shall we not receive evil? In all this did not Job sin with his lips."* (Job 2:10b)

Job struggled when the words of his wife and friends deflated his spirit. Job reached a point in his life where he said, *"Let the day perish wherein I was born, and the night in which it was said, There is a man child conceived."* (Job 3:3) Job also said, *"I have heard many such things: miserable comforters are ye all."* (Job 16:2) He later says in Job 16 that if he were in their position, that he would comfort with his words. He knew that these friends were weighing him down.

Spiritual Warfare Recognizes No Boundaries.

People who criticize in one area will criticize all areas. As Job's friends began to explain his plight, they opened up every area of his life to inspection. They talked about his marriage, his children, his business, his finances, and his health.

If you allow yourself one area of judgment, you will grant yourself the right to judge in all areas. You will be suspicious in all areas of life. You become the adversary to that person and discourage him. The discouraged one will begin to believe those words.

Reflecting on Your Position

How would people describe the spirit you give off? Are you Satan's mouthpiece? Are you doing his work for him? Do you criticize people's motives? Is it hard for you to be happy for someone who has greater success? Are you judging someone because you have a hidden sin and hope to put the spotlight on someone else before you are exposed?

ADVICE FOR THE CHRISTIAN ENGAGED IN SPIRITUAL WARFARE

Protect your spirit by filtering your eyes and ears. What you see and what you hear is what you speak. Acts 4:20 says, *"For we cannot but speak the things which we have seen and heard."* Our tongue is the mouthpiece for the eyes and the ears. If victory is found in controlling what you say, then you should be careful of that which you view and hear.

What you watch and hear develops and determines your spirit. You speak from the reservoir of words that are in your heart and mind. If you protect the gateways to your heart and mind, your reservoir will be pure. Why not listen to God's words more than you listen to the talk about other people?

Protect your spirit by containing your words. We filter our water, and we filter our air, but we don't filter our words. The greatest contamination in this world is not in the water we drink or in the air we breathe; it is in the words we think and say. If you would just speak less, you would prevent much warfare.

James 3:8 says, *"But the tongue can no man tame; it is an unruly evil, full of deadly poison."* The contamination of our words is poisonous. Every animal has been tamed, but the tongue is more unruly than every beast. Too often we find ourselves saying things that leak through. The words leaked through because they were never filtered out. Your best hope is to contain the tongue by filtering the mind. Philippians 4 teaches an eight-stage filtering process. HEPA filters can't filter one-hundred percent of allergens, but God's filter can take one-hundred percent of the impurity out of your words.

Philippians 4:8 says, *"Finally, brethren, whatsoever things are true, whatsoever things are honest, whatsoever things are just, whatsoever things are pure, whatsoever things are lovely, whatsoever things are of good report; if there be any virtue, and if there be any praise, think on these things."* When you want to think or say something, God wants you to think, "Is this true? Is this honest? Is this just? Is this pure? Is this lovely? Is this of good report? Does this contain any virtue? Is this praiseworthy?"

All of these filters are necessary to have a mature spirit, but you can start by developing one. Before you say anything, ask yourself, "Is this true?" Just start with one, or you will end up doing none. When the Bible says *"whatsoever things are true,"* it means truth according to the Bible. If you do not judge truth according to the Bible, then you become the judge of truth. A good or bad spirit is determined by how much Bible you know. To the extent that you know the Bible, you will control your spirit.

"Whatsoever things are lovely" is a great filter and easy to understand. We can say true things that are unlovely. The Pharisees brought to Jesus the woman taken in adultery. Their charges were true, but they were not lovely words to describe the fallen woman. Things that are lovely are things that are beautiful. The lovely filter might change what you watch on television, listen to on the radio, or read in the news.

The filters provide spiritual balance. You will have to face some ugly things in life. Some things can't be ignored. When faced with an ugly situation, counter with something lovely. When you hear a bad report, counter it with a lovely or true report about the person. This will protect your spirit and the spirit of those around you.

People mess up, but you can remind others of the good they have done. If a staff member made a terrible mistake, it would be easy to condemn him for the mistake. As a Christian I can prevent a negative spirit by saying kind things about the man who erred. I am to look for anything praiseworthy, of good report, or virtuous to say about him.

Find positive things to say about people. Romans 12:15 says, *"Rejoice with them that do rejoice, and weep with them that weep."* Praise and encourage when someone receives a blessing. You will boost your spirit when you encourage people.

Take one of these filters and use it this week. Study that word in the Scriptures. If you choose lovely, get a good definition for the word. Understand how this one filter can decide what you watch and hear and put in your mind.

Match your words with your thoughts. Don't be two-faced, saying one thing when you mean the opposite. If the words of your thoughts are negative, filter them out. Don't express your bad feelings. When you realize that something should not be spoken, assume that you shouldn't think about it either.

Don't criticize people's motives. Don't ask, "How come they have that position?" Don't say, "He only did this because…." Leave that work for Satan. When you ask such questions, you are giving him vacation time. Don't enviously ask, "What is he doing behind the scenes to be so successful?" Maybe God is richly blessing that person for righteousness. Envy doesn't seek for the truth. Envy seeks self-righteousness.

Stay completely away from motive judgments. Don't ask, "Why is he doing that?" Don't claim, "I know why he is doing that." God will judge everyone's motive. I Corinthians 3:13 says, *"Every man's work shall be made manifest: for the day shall declare it, because it shall be revealed by fire; and the fire shall try every man's work of what sort it is."* Allow Christ to determine the substance of everyone's works. Jeremiah 17:10 teaches that God will judge the interior motives of all men. Allow God to handle motives.

Chapter Two

Satan's Strategy

Satan's strategy for spiritual warfare has been so successful over the millennia that he has hidden his true agenda. Satan has led people to believe that satanic attacks involve the occult, Ouija boards, biting the heads off of bats to drink their blood, or rituals of animal sacrifice. None of these dark and bizarre events is the heart of Satanism, but the deceiver has tricked the world into believing these actions are at the core of his strategy.

Satan is like an expert boxer. He throws the world a fake jab with the left and brings a knock-out punch with the right. Satan's expertise in deception has hindered the world from identifying his devices. His plan is clever. His success is unquestionable.

Satan wants you to run scared from his reputation and never understand his real strategy. Understanding how Satan works is vital to defending his attacks and lining up your defenses.

When Satan is truly at work, you don't see him. His greatest success is when he is not visible. Satan does not want his influence to be apparent. Satan hides behind the scenes. He is a director of mischief, not an actor on the stage. Satan never seeks credit for his attacks. He wants you to blame another person or God.

To understand Satan's strategy, you have to understand what his name means. The Greek word for Satan is *diabolos*, which sounds like the English word "diabolic." *Diabolos* is a compound Greek word composed of the words *dia*, which means "through," and *ballow*, which means "to throw." The word means "to throw through." In our vernacular, we would say that Satan is trying to drive a wedge, or Satan is trying to divide us.

The antonym of *diabolos* is "symbolic." *Symbolic* is a compound Greek word composed of *syn*, which means "together," and *ballow*. *Symbolic* means "to throw together." Symbols pull people together.

The American flag and the Cross are two strong examples of symbols. The American flag is a symbol revered by most Americans regardless of their race, age, or politics. People are bothered when someone is burning the flag or using one to wash a car because the perpetrators are dividing the symbol from the object for which it stands. The Cross is revered by Christians as a symbol of the Lord Jesus Christ. The Cross is a reminder of our purpose in fulfilling the Great Commission. The Cross reminds us of suffering, salvation, and eternal life.

Satanic warfare is being waged by dividing and separating what once had symbolism or togetherness. Satanic attacks can be recognized by the resulting division of things that God has put together.

Satan's Strategy: Divide the Relationships That God Has Ordained.

The command to put on the full armor of God is given in Ephesians 6:11-19. The full armor of God enables you to stand against Satan's methods. The preceding passage (Ephesians 5:18-6:10) instructs you on how to conduct six different relationships. These two passages are consecutive because God instructs you to put on His armor to defend against Satan's attacks against these relationships. When you mention spiritual warfare, you are referring to Satan's attacks against the following six relationships:

1. The relationship between a person and God
2. A person's relationship with himself
3. The relationship between spouses
4. The relationship between parents and children
5. The relationship between employers and employees
6. The relationship between brothers and sisters in Christ.

God ordained these six relationships to provide security and stability to mankind. The stability of a society is measured by the strength of the six ordained relationships. Churches, families, and places of employment all bring stability to a society. Your relationships are in the crosshairs of Satan because he can promote insecurity and instability through the absence of healthy relationships.

Spiritual warfare pits you against others or even yourself. A mid-life crisis comes when a person evaluates his life and is disappointed by his past and his level of success. Spiritual warfare is pitting you against yourself and darkening your heart. Satanism gets you to lack confidence, doubt yourself, and believe your problems are centered around you. Satanism attempts to divide you from God.

The greatest satanic influence in our country is the destruction of the home. Couples considering divorce are under satanic attack because they contemplate dividing a relationship that God has ordained. The devil would like to redefine marriage and allow same-gender marriages because these drive a wedge into God's original intent for marriage.

God instituted the church, so church members who leave their church have been defeated in spiritual warfare. When people are driven from the local church, it hurts the body of Christ. Satan works hard to instill hurt feelings and bad blood between church members. Satan drives the wedge of pride and envy that divides church members.

Satan's Strategy: Search for Vulnerability

The Iliad by Homer tells the story of Achilles. When Achilles was born, his mother, Thetis, dipped him in the river Styx to make him immortal. Thetis held Achilles' heel to dip him in the river, so his heel never received the immortal powers of the river. Achilles was the bravest, the most handsome, the quickest, and the most able warrior that besieged Troy during the Trojan War, but none of those attributes protected his weak spot. Achilles was killed when Paris' arrow struck him in the heel—his vulnerable spot—during the Trojan War. Achilles didn't die because of sin; he died because he had a vulnerable spot that was exploited.

Satan is aiming for your Achilles heel. Some of Satan's arrows might bounce off of you as though you are immortal. He can handle temporary failures because he is patiently testing for your vulnerable spot.

He does not march against you with the forces of Hell; he uses the back-door strategy. He shoots you from behind; he shoots you in the heel. He lurks in the blind spots unseen in your rearview mirror. He scouts the vulnerable spots in your marriage, family, and pleasures. The weakest family member and the most vulnerable stages of life will be attacked.

Satan is like an expert boxer who tries to hit a wound. If the opponent's left eye is cut, a good boxer will jab at the left eye because it is vulnerable. Satan uses the same principle. He is searching for the vulnerable spots of the people within a relationship. When he discovers those vulnerabilities, he will attack them.

Reflecting on Your Position

Do you feel that there is division in your life? How are your God-ordained relationships? Are you casting blame on other people in your God-ordained relationships? Have you considered that others may not be your problem? Have you considered that your problems might stem from Satan's driving wedges in your God-ordained relationships?

ADVICE TO THE CHRISTIAN ENGAGED IN SPIRITUAL WARFARE

Don't fight people. All of your relationships are with people, but you must realize that your struggles are not against people. Satan wants you to incorrectly think that your problem is with another person. Ephesians 6:12 says, *"For we wrestle not against flesh and blood...."* You do not wrestle against men. You do not wrestle with your parent, child, employer, employee, or spouse.

Your battle is against the satanic forces that are negatively influencing these six relationships. You wrestle *"...against principalities, against powers, against the rulers of the darkness of this world, against spiritual wickedness in high places."* Victory in spiritual warfare will come when you stop fighting the wrong enemy—those people in your God-ordained relationships—and correctly fight the powers of spiritual wickedness.

Don't underestimate Satan. A subsequent chapter in this book will teach how to respond to spiritual attacks, but you cannot fight the devil. The Bible warns you to be cognizant of Satan's devices. He is the prince of this world; his arsenal is more powerful than you. If he is the source of your problems, you must learn the proper combat techniques.

Don't overestimate Satan. Matthew 4 says that it was the Spirit who led Jesus into the wilderness to be tempted of the devil. When Satan is our adversary, God has allowed him to be so. Satan is no match for God. Matthew 4 is not a demonstration of how Satan works; the passage demonstrates how Christ was and will be victorious over Satan.

When God has allowed Satan to mess with a man, it has always with been His permission. God allowed Satan to bring problems to Job. God told Satan what he could touch and what he could not touch. As evil as the devil is, he cannot go beyond what God allows. The devil is not a counterpart to God. There is no one like God. Satan was created by God; he is no match for our Heavenly Father.

Learn to discern. The problems brought about by Satan are very different than the problems brought about by God or by you. Discerning the spirits can be hard, but the Bible commands us to discern. A later chapter takes up this topic. As you learn to recognize the source of your problems, you will learn to properly direct your defenses.

Chapter Three

Satan's Greatest Success Story

Since the creation of man, Satan has waged war against God-ordained relationships and searched for the vulnerabilities in those relationships. Satan's toughest conquest was his first—the victory over Adam and Eve. He conquered a couple who had all of their needs met by God. The garden was a paradise that contained no solicitation of evil. The human nature of Adam and Eve had not been warped by the worries, frustrations, and failures of life. By deceiving Adam and Eve, Satan essentially sold a bag of ice to an Eskimo.

Genesis 3 records that Satan waged his attack against Eve. I Timothy 2:14 teaches that Eve was deceived. Adam was not deceived because he had the security of God-given dominion. Women can be as smart and wise as men, but they are more vulnerable to deception.

Satan discovered Eve's susceptibility to deception and

attacked her vulnerabilities. He discovered her Achilles heel. Eve's weaknesses weren't sinful, but her vulnerability was the portal that Satan used to bring sin into the world. Vulnerabilities are not always sinful areas because Eve was vulnerable when there was not yet sin in the Garden.

Satan Attacked Eve's Relationship With God.

Satan will attempt to divide a God-ordained relationship. He first attacked the relationship between Eve and God. Satan questioned what God said when he said, "...*Yea, hath God said, Ye shall not eat of every tree of the garden?*"

Eve responded with God's words. "...*We may eat of the fruit of the trees of the garden: But of the fruit of the tree which is in the midst of the garden, God hath said, Ye shall not eat of it, neither shall ye touch it, lest ye die.*"

Satan questioned the authority that Eve had given God in her life. "...*Ye shall not surely die: For God doth know that in the day ye eat thereof, then your eyes shall be opened, and ye shall be as gods, knowing good and evil.*"

Satan drove his wedge between God and Eve. He told Eve that God was withholding good things and the ability to be like God. Satan questioned God's motive in forbidding her and Adam to eat from the tree.

Satan Probed the Vulnerability in Eve's Appetites.

Satan exploited an undisciplined appetite possessed by Eve. Eating food is mentioned several times in the conversation between the serpent and Eve. Eating food is not sinful, but the undisciplined appetite for a particular food led to Eve's sin.

Few people will make a violent U-turn to be uncharacteristically malicious. Satan knows that we will take small steps that encroach upon our appetites. We like little indulgences.

My opinion is that Adam and Eve might have been on a tasting expedition in the garden of Eden once they were permitted to eat from the trees. I would imagine that a newly created being with thousands of options for eating would exercise his taste buds. If it were me, I would have wanted to try every fruit available.

There were fruits and flavors on those trees that we could never imagine. Our senses are dulled by sin. *"For now we see through a glass, darkly"*; we experience shadows of the future reality in a glorified body. Their sensory ability was more heightened than our abilities. I believe that Adam and Eve did more than taste the fruit when they ate it. They enjoyed eating with senses that we do not possess.

Perhaps Satan saw the rapid way they were indulging their senses and saw the potential for vulnerability. The serpent said that the fruit would make one wise and appealed to a different sense than taste. Eve believed that the fruit would fulfill another appetite she had—a desire to be wise. Satan used that desire against her to bring victory.

Satan Probed Eve's Vulnerability Stemming From Feelings of Deprivation.

Satan fed and then exploited Eve's desire to have what God forbade. Satan knows that people are susceptible in areas where they feel cheated. He knows that people will validate their sin with the injustice they perceive against them.

Eve knew that God had told Adam not to eat from the tree of the knowledge of good and evil, and she knew that the punishment was death. Satan countered by saying that God was keeping something from her. He claimed that God was depriving her of the tree because it would open her eyes (he was appealing to her senses) and give her knowledge of good and evil. Eve was convinced that eating the fruit would fulfill the desires of which she was deprived.

Satan Probed Eve's Vulnerability Stemming From a Desire for Power and Dominion.

Satan appealed to the desire for power and dominion when he said, *"Ye shall be as gods."* Adam received dominion over God's creation in Genesis 2. Adam and Eve proved the cliché "absolute power corrupts absolutely." When Adam and Eve received power from God, they wanted a little bit more. People who are not satisfied with God's provision will accept whatever Satan offers.

Reflecting on Your Position

Where is Satan driving a wedge in your God-ordained relationships? To which of your appetites is Satan appealing? Are you using sin to compensate in the areas where you feel deprived? Are you struggling with a desire for power and dominion? Do you continue to focus on what you cannot fix? What signs have you shown the devil to convince him that you and God don't agree? When Satan whispers, "You don't have to do it God's way," do you consider if that is true?

ADVICE TO THE CHRISTIAN ENGAGED IN SPIRITUAL WARFARE

Keep an open mind, eyes, and heart in the discovery of vulnerable areas. Understand the vulnerable situations and times of life for you and loved ones. Let the Word of God, the preaching of the Bible, and fellow Christians show you your blind spots. Seek the advice of an older guide who can lead you through weak times. Watch for family members and loved ones who might be under attack. Satan might be waging war on you through them because they are more vulnerable.

Be aware of the times when appetites are heightened. Undisciplined appetites are not restricted to foods. Everyone is vulnerable in different areas. Three stages in life are most vulnerable—adolescence, single adulthood, and early married life.

Children are vulnerable because they constantly perceive new feelings. Hormone development changes the behavior of adolescents and teenagers. Exposure to new senses can become a time of calamity for many teenagers if they are not able to corral those emotions during this time of growth.

Young singles are vulnerable when they gain independence because they tend to experiment and produce regrets, scars, and stains. Satan wages a war on their vulnerability to the vices they have yet to see, much like Satan appealed to Eve's desire to know things which were previously forbidden.

Many young singles have ruined their sexuality and think it is dirty, when they should have learned that sexuality is sacred and precious. The average age for a man to get married is at twenty-eight years old, and by then he has had seven sex partners. Every time he gave himself sexually to somebody else, he lost a little part of him that he could not give to his wife. His experimentation has trashed the sacredness and symbol of marriage. This is a spiritual victory for the devil.

Young married couples are vulnerable because they are so obsessed with their marriage that they backslide from God. They are like Adam and Eve who are on a tasting spree in the garden of Eden. Marriage opens up possibilities for people to taste paradise, but they forget their Christianity. It is not uncommon for a married couple to skip church for six months.

Stop asking God why you can't have things. If you don't count your blessings, you will be discontent with those blessings.

The natural, sinful tendency is to feel that God has forbidden what you think you should possess. The Devil convinced Eve that God had deprived her of the blessing of having the knowledge of God.

God has no intention of explaining everything. What He wants to reveal about Himself has been revealed in the Bible. He might reveal more about Himself in Heaven someday, but for now, there's only so much knowledge that we can have. The bottom line is that God hasn't explained His reason for depriving us. God might explain His reasons, but that will never be required of Him.

Satan is probing for the weak faith that questions God. Satan discovers vulnerability when we feel we have a right to know the reasons why. When we agree with Satan, we have become fertile soil for the seed of bitterness that springs up and defiles us. Eve should have said, "No, Satan. There are just some things I'll have to live without knowing."

Whether you feel deprived of power or possessions, God wants you to trust Him without knowing all of the answers. When you fret about what you cannot fix, you are vulnerable to Satan's attacks. Instead, focus on what God has done for you and improve the opportunities He has provided.

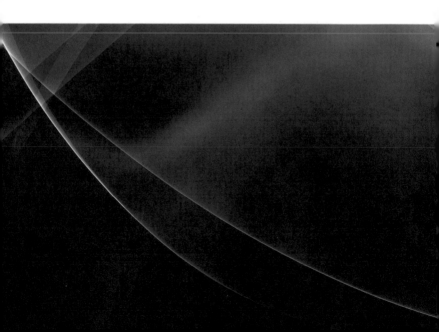

Section Two

SATAN'S BATTLE PLAN

Chapter 4

Satan's Blueprint

Satan's efforts against a man are generic. The same plan he had to defeat Adam and Eve is the same plan he uses against you. His efforts are like the machinery in an assembly line. They are the same processes performed on another piece that will hopefully yield the same product. You are that piece that Satan wants to press, stamp, and cast into a die that yields a disabled Christian.

Step One: Satan Probes You Until He Finds a Weakness.

Satan examines you. You do not know how watched you are. You think you can shut the lights off and live in your secret world. You can sin in private and think that nobody sees you, but you are observed by beings about which you don't want to know. They study your patterns and habits, probing and looking for areas of vulnerability. The Devil has a database on your likes and dislikes. He does a better job of tracking conversations than the cellular phone company. He has a list of what you like to talk about. He knows your hobbies, weaknesses, and flaws. He is waiting for the pattern to develop.

He will test you with every temptation. Your reaction is important to him. He wants to know what races your heart or turns your head. If you are a decent Christian, you will not yield to many of his tests. However, he knows that you will yield to something, and he will bide his time until it is discovered. He wants you to form a habit. He wants you to obtain an addiction. You might not fall for alcohol, cocaine, or pornography, but you might be enticed by displays of pride and sins of the tongue. Everyone has areas that turn them on. Satan is trying to ignite yours.

Your fears are in his file. He knows what will paralyze you. He knows what traumatic experiences molded your life. Satan yearns to use the fears of a molestation victim to injure the victim's marriage. He watches a child cringe in fear. He watches a child hide in the corner. He sees him lock up the door of his heart and say, "I'm never bringing that out again." Satan laughs, knowing that he will use that fear in a few decades. He will be certain that it revisits that child who grows up.

Your unguarded moments are observed. Patiently he waits for you to leave open the door of your heart or mind. He wants to catch you when you are not walking circumspectly. Your gaze is followed. He tunes in to the frequency of your heart. He observes what makes you pause and consider. He listens to what your ears detect. He waits for the object that makes you say, "Wow!" He considers how he can then entice your heart with the trinket. He is curious about your curiosities. He is desirous to know your desires. He is the fisherman who is considering what lure or what bait to put on the hook.

Step Two: Satan Victimizes.

He offers you excuses. He suggests acceptable reasons to indulge in sin:

"You were hurt as a child."

"Your wife is not treating you very well right now. She is refusing your affection."

"Your husband isn't taking care of you. He is out with somebody else. He has abandoned his vows. Why shouldn't you abandon your vows?"

The excuses he offers build a logical plan in your mind. You agree with him:

"It's okay if I watch this."

"I deserve to listen to this."

"Smoking this, sniffing that, and drinking a lot will deliver me from this unfair pain."

"I can cheat since my spouse is cheating."

The deep, dark secrets of your life are used against you. Through clever manipulation and keen observation, a dangerous enemy gains access to the inner parts that you would not even reveal to your best friends.

Step Three: Satan Increases His Territory Through Your Sins.

Satan now has access to you. These sins were doorways for his influence to enter. The sins are leverage that he uses to further paralyze you.

Most Bible students don't believe that a saved person can be possessed of a demon because possession requires ownership. Saved people are owned by Jesus Christ; however, the saved person can yield territory to a devil until he is living like a devil. A Christian can get to the point where he is listening to and obeying devils.

Ephesians 4:27 says, *"Neither give place to the devil."* Place is translated from the Greek word *topos*, which is a root for the English word *topography*. Giving place to the devil means that you yield ground and territory. You are like an army that is being pushed back by the advancing enemy.

Satan cannot forcibly take territory from you. He can only take what you give to him. His methods therefore must be filled with guile. He enters like a Trojan horse: you think it's a gift, but it is your destruction. Satan is powerful, but his power in your life is to the extent that you open a door and allow him to enter.

The sins that he leads you to commit are weapons in his spiritual warfare. They are the tools of Hell. Your indulgences damage your spirit, wreck your attitude, destroy your marriage, and destroy your home. If it is just a white powder you sniff, then why is it destroying God's ordained relationships? If it's just a material dollar bill at the casino, why is strife brought to your family when you can't pay the mortgage because you wasted your money at the casino? If beer is just a brown liquid in a brown bottle, why do people risk their lives to get behind a wheel and drive? Why does it destroy jobs and families and marriages? If it was just a little rendezvous on the side, why does it bring shame to children, destroy a marriage, and reproach a family? If it is just music, why did it influence the Columbine killers? If it's just music, why does it entice so many people to fornicate? If it's just music, why do addicts confess that they cannot properly hallucinate without the presence of certain rock music.

These sins are weapons in spiritual warfare because they are not simply physical deeds you commit with your body. These are spiritual relationships you commit with the devil, and ultimately, these sins keep you from your God-ordained relationships.

Reconsider the case of alcohol. It has broken up marriages. It has killed family members. It has cost people jobs. It has caused pastors to leave the pulpit and divide churches. The shame of it keeps the drunk from confessing his sin to God. All of these results drive a wedge in your relationships.

Satan sets up shop in your heart. He builds a fort inside of your home. He builds a spiritual factory that produces pollution. Your thoughts and feelings become contaminated. You become a cesspool of iniquity, justify sin, and blame God for your problems.

Step Four: Satan Waits for Your Sins to Make You Feel Despondent.

Once you give place to the devil, you will find yourself repeatedly and habitually engaging in your sin. You feel helpless and defeated. Your decisions are harmful and destructive. Satan knows that you will try another sin to compensate for your helplessness.

Step Five: Satan Once Again Expands His Territory.

When you give Satan an inch, he wants to take it a mile. However, he will take one inch at a time as long as he is making progress.

Cocaine addicts will often tell you that they started with marijuana. Most people won't go straight to cocaine because it is a harder drug and carries greater risks. Marijuana doesn't seem as bad; it has less stigma than cocaine. Once you smoke marijuana, you will justify that it has not harmed you. If Satan can get you to smoke marijuana, he has gotten you closer to sniffing cocaine. If you justified that marijuana wasn't as bad as you thought it would be, then cocaine probably isn't as bad as its reputation either. This is how Satan pummels you one inch at a time.

The first sin was a stepping stone. Satan wants to take you to greater heights of sin. He is expanding his territory to ensure that you are exposed to every vice that might destroy you.

Step Six: Satan Sends You Down the Hill of Destruction.

There is a common road that Satan wants us to travel. The road is downhill so you can coast. The road ends with no warning and drops you off a precipice.

He takes your desire and offers you a distraction with that desire. He uses a distraction to disrupt life's rhythm. The disruption leads to dependence. You need your sin. You must have it. Dozens of times you have said, "I can quit anytime I want to," but you are still indulging.

You descend into the abyss and become an impotent Christian. You are destroyed because of one area where you give place to the Devil. The pride is so strong that you will not seek help.

Satan once again victimizes you as you swirl in the vicious cycle of justifying that you need another fix of another sin to soothe the pain. The Devil will once again expand his territory.

Reflecting on Your Position

What does Satan's file about you say? What does Satan observe you listening to and watching? What are your appetites? What are the things that you enjoy doing? What are your likes and dislikes? What are your pleasures? What is it that you do in secret when nobody is watching?

ADVICE TO THE CHRISTIAN ENGAGED IN SPIRITUAL WARFARE

Don't give place to the devil. Satan's power was stripped at an old rugged Cross. The empty tomb reminds him of pending defeat. He is just a loud roar until you allow him access. He has great power amongst those who grant it to him. Satan only has power over you to the extent you allow.

When you give place to the devil, you create a permanent breaking point upon which Satan will aim his artillery. Matthew 12 talks about an unclean spirit who was expelled from a person. He later returns with seven spirits who are more wicked than himself. The end result is worse because the attack intensifies. Once you cross the line of experimentation and experiencing, you have created a fissure into which the Devil can drive his wedges.

Chapter 5

Discerning the Enemy

The Bible warns in II Corinthians 2:11, *"Lest Satan should get an advantage of us: for we are not ignorant of his devices."* To gain an understanding of what Satan attacks, we also need to learn how Satan attacks. Spiritual warfare is about driving a wedge in our God-ordained relationships through the crack of our vulnerabilities. We cannot be ignorant of Satan's weapons that enable him to drive a wedge.

The weapons of Satan are exposed to us in the Scriptures. This is one reason why Satan would like to distract you from the Bible and lead you to believe that it is boring. He wants you to be ignorant of what he is doing in your life.

As I study the Bible, I look for patterns of Satan at work. I look for the stories of men and women who have lost to Satan and have also been victorious. I look for patterns. The fall of Adam and Eve is an example of failure upon which we can model a success. We can see the fingerprints of Satan and match those to his fingerprints when they show up in our lives.

Satan Divides By Strife, Confusion, and Fear.

James 3:16 says, *"For where envying and strife is, there is confusion and every evil work."* Hebrews 2:14-15 says, *"Forasmuch then as the children are partakers of flesh and blood, he [Jesus Christ] also himself likewise took part of the same; that through death he might destroy him that had the power of death, that is, the devil; And deliver them who through fear of death were all their lifetime subject to bondage."*

Satan wants you to be afraid because fear paralyzes you. Strife between people is a strong wedge in a relationship. It keeps you from standing with your friends. God is not the author of confusion; Satan is the author. Anytime you are confused, afraid, and fighting, you cannot accomplish the work of God.

Satan Divides With False Substitutes

The Greek New Testament word for *devil* means "demonize." *Demonization* is the distribution of fortunes or predictions, and refers to items that are substitutes or trinkets. Satan wants to give you a substitute treasure. This type of weapon of Satan is an inferior product that is more glitzy than the real deal.

Addictions form when people accept a substitute for God's provision. The high value that an addict places on a substitute treasure causes the object to become an idol. The addict will do anything in order to keep his substitute treasure because he cannot live without his idol.

A recent ad campaign for a local cable television provider illustrates idolatry. In the ads, a person says that he would rather do something he dreads than give up his cable television. One ad insinuates that a man is driving naked in his car. The man says, "I'd rather drive naked than give up my cable." Another advertisement shows a woman with her ex-husband next to her. She says, "I'd rather get back with my ex than give up my cable." The people in the advertisements are addicts because they say, "I cannot live without something." I'm not accusing the cable company of demonizing, but their ad executives appeal to the idolatry of television.

Satan's substitutes are false relationships that artificially salve your wounds. The twenty-first century is filled with the artificial relationships of electronics. People relate better to their televisions and cell phones and Internet than they do to their God-ordained relationships. Many have accepted Satan's substitutes.

Satan Divides With Bitterness.

The development of bitterness is a sign that you are under satanic attack. If you shake your fist at God during and after a tragedy, you can be assured that Satan is cheering you on. Bitterness is the influence of Satan driving a wedge between you and God. Your bitterness comes when you believe Satan's lies. He tells you that someone must take the blame, so you place the blame on God.

Satan Divides With Accusations and Suspicions.

The Devil works to plant skeptical thoughts in your mind. He works on your pride and wants you to ask, "What right does someone have to do that to me?"

Satan is the accuser of the brethren. He influences you to be suspicious of your spouse or parents. Satan whispers in your ear that you should be wary of your co-workers and fellow church members. Suspicion is the crime-scene evidence that Satan was involved.

Suspicion destroys confidence in other people. Suspicions can destroy a marriage relationship when no trespass was committed. Spouses should be slow to suspect because they took a vow to stay with their spouse no matter what happens. Suspicions war against those vows.

The attacks against Job began with the loss of many relationships and all of his material possessions. Satan then disappeared from the remainder of the book. Job had proven that his faith was not in his material possessions, so Satan attacked his relationships from behind the scenes. The book of Job is rife with accusations and suspicions from his three friends. Job's wife said to curse God and die. His friends eventually broke off their relationship with him. They looked for the cause and effect between Job's life and tragedies. They concluded that Job must have been a wicked man—an unfair accusation. Their statements were suspicious barbs against an undeserving man.

Satan Attacks Material Possessions.

Loss of material possessions is another mark of satanic work. The story of Job shows that Satan requested that God remove Job's material possessions. Satan claimed that these possessions were why Job feared God, and God allowed Satan to touch Job's possessions.

When Job proved that his possessions were not the cause of his affection toward God, Satan asked for permission to touch Job's health. It is the permissive will of God to allow Satan to strip you of that which brings you security. At some point in your life, Satan is going to shake your confidence. He is going to find out if your confidence is in your checkbook, in your vehicle, in your wardrobe, or in your home.

Satan Attacks Through Envy.

Envy has defeated more Christians than any other single sin. Envy is Satan's "go-to" sin. Satan loves for envy to flare in your heart; it is a most formidable weapon. Envy has three parts: (1) discontentment; (2) resentment of what other people have; (3) a longing for what other people have.

Envy is a feeling caused by someone else. The rise of envy is not the fault of the other person, but the other person stirs up those feelings. This is similar to how the smell of food reminds you that you should be hungry.

When Satan can't mislead you with the appetites of your flesh, he leads you to resentful feelings and thoughts that say, "Hey! I don't have that." The tendency to look at people and see what they have gives rise to envy.

The book of Proverbs provides several warnings to refrain from envy (Proverbs 3:31; 23:17; 24:1, 19). Proverbs 14:30 teaches, *"A sound heart is the life of the flesh: but envy the rottenness of the bones."* Envy is one of the surest ways to end up in poverty, under judgment, or in trouble with the Lord.

Satan attempted to destroy the nation of Israel with envy. Israel always was in the crosshairs of Satan because it was a physical tool that God used to perform his supernatural work on the earth. The Jews produced the Messiah and the Bible. Satan's desire to destroy Israel is immense.

Envy moved Joseph's brothers to plot his murder and sell him into slavery. Joseph proved that God has great power to overturn the wicked designs of evil people, but nonetheless the evil still was there. God used this problem for good, but Joseph still had to struggle with the rejection of his family, being taken from his home, being lied about by Potiphar's wife, and spending time in prison. All of these problems were the result of his brothers' envy.

The Gospel of Matthew teaches that Christ was betrayed and put on the Cross due to the envy of the Sadducees and Pharisees. These Jewish leaders were insecure because of Jesus' presence.

Our Lord was a threat to their power. Mark 15:10 says that Pontius Pilate *"...knew that the chief priests had delivered him* [Jesus] *for envy."*

The Sadducees and Pharisees didn't love Jesus Christ. They had no relationship with Jesus. They deeply resented that He would have the power they desired. They felt He was unqualified. They questioned His qualifications and asked where He went to school. They became infected with resentment and conspired to kill Him.

Envy can easily arise in marriages. If you think your friend has a better marriage, Satan will whisper in your ear, "If you were married to his or her spouse, you would be happy like them." Envy arises when you believe that your friend is happy because he has a better spouse than you.

Similar feelings arise with children. Some people resent that they cannot have children. Other people resent that the children of others turned out better than their own children. Barren couples think, "I would be happy if I just had children." Parents think, "I would be happy if I had their children." Christians can become envious over the success of others within a ministry. Pastors think, "If I just had his church. If I only had his church members, I could be as successful. If I only had the offerings that his church had, then I could build a great work." All of these thoughts are envious. Envy is ultimately a failure to see God's grace in another person's life.

Satan's suggestions are the arrows with which he is probing you. After several years of stability in marriage, a job, or a church, he asks, "Are you as happy as you thought you'd be?" Satan asks, "Are you as content with that spouse as you dreamed of being when you were engaged?" Dwelling on those questions opens the door to satanic attack.

Reflecting on Your Position

Have you unwittingly become an agent for Satan? Have you bought his lies? Have you indulged in sinful deeds that Satan wants because you are trying to handle your insecurities? Do you bring addictions into your life that drive their own wedges?

What cheap substitutes are you pursuing? What would you rather have than a relationship with God? What would you rather have than your Bible? What would you rather have than a relationship with your spouse? Are you dreaming of an affair? What would you rather have than a relationship with your mom or dad? What would you rather have than your church? What would you rather have than a Christian testimony?

Where is your bitterness? For what do you cast blame on God? Do you say, "How can God expect me to have a happy marriage? Look at whom He gave me for a spouse." Are you failing to see the grace of God in the lives of others?

ADVICE TO THE CHRISTIAN ENGAGED IN SPIRITUAL WARFARE

Cast down imaginations. II Corinthians 10:3-6 addresses a defense in spiritual warfare. *"For though we walk in the flesh, we do not war after the flesh: (For the weapons of our warfare are not carnal, but mighty through God to the pulling down of strong holds;) Casting down imaginations, and every high thing that exalteth itself against the knowledge of God, and bringing into captivity every thought to the obedience of Christ; And having in a readiness to revenge all disobedience, when your obedience is fulfilled."*

Satan works best with emotions and feelings rather than facts and truth. He is focused on manipulating your emotions. Your heart feels emotions that are by-products of your thoughts. All authority that Satan has in your life is authority you have given to him. You will allow feelings of resentment to rise up inside of you. You will allow the resentment to turn into despising and hatred. Casting down imaginations requires you to push away the thoughts that injure your relationship with God and those in God-ordained relationships. You will not stop thoughts from coming into your mind, but you can keep them from staying—just like you can't help who comes and knocks on your front door, but you can control who comes into your house. You choose whether or not you entertain the thought that leads to discontentment.

Cast down imaginations with Scriptures. Memorize II Corinthians 10:5 and quote it to yourself when you are contemplating the enjoyment of unrealistic thoughts. Memorize Psalm 119:113, "*I hate vain thoughts: but thy law do I love.*" Quote this Scripture to yourself until it is in your heart. Think about what God's law says about the words you want to speak about those you envy.

Counter your thoughts of envy with Scriptural truths. If you fret about your future, think on Philippians 1:6, "*Being confident of this very thing, that he which hath begun a good work in you will perform it until the day of Jesus Christ.*" When you worry that you will never amount to much, remember that God promised to perform the work in you until He comes back.

Renew your faith in the sovereignty of God. God is in control, and nobody gets ahead because of his past, and nobody is hindered because of his past. Your potential is found in your current commitment to Christ. Your past should make your heart tender toward Jesus Christ because you look upon his grace and mercy in preparing you for today.

My past taught me there is a great God. My past taught me that my Father in Heaven loves me. My past taught me that God is a forgiving God. My past taught me that the Bible is true. My past taught me that I can trust my authorities, including my parents and pastor. My past taught me that the Word of God is the best place to spend my life.

Your past might have made you bitter against the will of God, but your past has not hindered you; bitterness hindered you. People with bad pasts have used that past to avoid the track that others have taken. Proverbs 22:3 says, *"A prudent man foreseeth the evil, and hideth himself: but the simple pass on, and are punished."* People with bad pasts can decide that they won't taste the world anymore because it is a dry, empty lifestyle.

We fight the feelings that cause us to question whether or not we can trust God. If I believe that God is in control, I follow His lead. If I don't trust His sovereignty, I stray from His paths. When the devil whispers in your ear, "If only you were married to her…," your faith in the sovereignty of God says, "God put my wife and me together. God knew what I needed even more than I knew what I needed." Faith and trust in God's sovereignty believes that wherever you are and whatever you are is exactly what God intends.

You are susceptible to envy as long as your mind is opened to the Devil's whispers that God has led you down a lesser path that does not fulfill your potential. How much time do you spend daydreaming of how life could be if you had different circumstances? The daydreaming is the gateway into your heart for lust, covetousness, and envy.

You will be as happy and content as you decide to be. The gap between your contentment and where the Devil says you could be is the battleground. He owns it when you open the door to his attacks.

Section Three

THE BATTLEGROUND

Chapter Six

When Satan Is Not the Problem

Before a soldier retaliates, he should first know who attacked him. Everyone knows when they are in the battle, but many people cannot discern who launched an attack against them. Distinguishing between attacks launched by Satan and a test from God is important. What some people believe is spiritual warfare might be a problem brought about by themselves or by God. Before you launch a grenade, you better know where you are throwing it.

When the Twin Towers were knocked down on September 11, Americans wanted action. President Bush's approval ratings were extremely high; Democrats and Republicans passed bipartisan legislation to defend America. One question that had to be answered was, "Who is responsible for this?" America understood that Al Qaeda was responsible, but would retaliation mean that we would attack Afghanistan? Were we at war with someone other than the hijackers? Would retaliation involve a war in Iraq?

Was Saddam Hussein behind this? Would retaliation involve an offensive against Iran? As the Iraq War has dominated politics in the first decade of the twenty-first century, war's opponents have asked, "Why did we go there in the first place?" and "Were they the ones responsible for September 11?" The enemy is not always clearly defined.

This book is not an opinion of the Iraq War, but current events illustrate a definition problem. Before a person claims that he is under satanic attack, he needs to evaluate the source of his problem. Problems that enter our life have three sources: ourselves, God, or satanic opposition. Satan is not always the source of your problems. The wise Christian will investigate and discern the source of his problem before he declares the enemy to be Satan or a fellow human being. The Christian who considers the problems that war against his spirit needs to answer two questions:

What is the source of this problem?

Why did this problem come to me?

If you could find the truthful answer to these questions, you might realize that you are one of the greatest sources of problems in your life. Satan gets a lot of blame for the problems we make in our own lives. Instead of reacting to a problem with introspection, we point fingers at Satan and other people. You need to be honest and first see if you are the cause of your problems.

Do You Bring Problems Upon Yourself Because of Ignorance?

Hosea 4:6 says, "*My people are destroyed for lack of knowledge....*" Ignorance is a lack of knowledge. Many problems find their root in ignorance.

A fellow pastor told me a story of being pulled over by a police officer when he was returning from a speaking engagement. The pastor said that he picked his own speed because there were no posted speed limit signs on the roads. When the state trooper approached the car, the pastor said, "Officer, why are you pulling me over?"

The trooper replied, "Because you were speeding."

The pastor said, "Officer, I noticed this entire county has an absence of posted speed limit signs."

"You are right," the officer replied. "There are no posted speed limit signs in this county, and that is by design. We don't want to clutter up the highway."

The pastor questioned, "How am I supposed to know how fast I can drive?"

"In the state record books, the speed limit for this county is recorded."

The pastor argued, "Why would I want to read that?"

"To avoid what you are getting right now," the trooper answered as he wrote the ticket.

The pastor did not argue any further. He chatted for several moments with the trooper and talked about how he was a preacher. The trooper then asked the preacher, "How many of your people know what the Bible says?"

Transparently, the pastor replied, "Far too few of them know what the Bible says." The trooper's question convicted the pastor.

"But it's still in the Book, isn't it? When they stand before your God in judgment, will ignorance be an acceptable defense?"

Knowing he was had, the pastor replied, "Can I just have my ticket so that I can go?"

So few people have read the Constitution, but it still governs our lives. So few people have read the entire tax code, but they will be penalized if they break it. A person is governed by these laws regardless of his level of knowledge or ignorance. Whether you stand before a local judge, a law officer, or God, ignorance is not an acceptable defense.

A problem with ignorance is that people enjoy ignorance because they believe they are not accountable. People will deceive themselves and say, "I didn't know that," in order to justify their self-inflicted problems.

God doesn't accept ignorance as an excuse. People suffer through problems in life because they do not apply a Biblical solution to their problem. People who have never read a Bible still live under the same physical and moral laws as the utmost Bible scholar. Ignorance will not be an excuse for failing to accept Christ's salvation. Hell will be populated with people who were ignorant of Christ's free gift of salvation as well as with people who knowingly rejected salvation.

You bring problems rooted in ignorance on yourself when you permit yourself to do what is not permissible instead of restricting yourself to what is permissible. Allow me to illustrate with a mistake from my childhood.

Holland, Michigan, was not an urban environment. My home was in the midst of a corn field. When I stepped out of my house, I could see corn, farms, and farm animals. I grew up with guns. I played plenty of sports with my friends, but our playtime included hunting.

On one particular in-season day, my friends and I headed down a dirt road with our shotguns in tow. We thought we were on public property; thus, we were giving ourselves permission to hunt on this property. "No hunting" and "No trespassing" signs were absent. None of my friends had ever investigated whether it was okay to travel on this dirt road and go hunting. We assumed we could go hunting because no one had said that we could not go hunting in the area.

We entered the tall weeds and started looking for game. That perfect silence for hunting was ruined by a pickup truck that barreled down the road. The driver locked up the brakes, turned the truck sideways, and jumped out of the truck with a double-barrel shotgun pointed at me! He said, "Get off of my land!"

I said, "Who are you?"

He said, "The guy that is about to shoot you."

"My name is Jack Schaap." I slowly walked toward him and extended my hand.

"I don't want to shake your hand. I want you off my land."

I had returned to the road and said, "I am off your land now."

The landowner replied, "That's not good enough for me; you were on my land. The county sheriff will be here in a few minutes."

The county sheriff came and took the guns from everyone in my group. I had a six-hundred-dollar shotgun, and I fumed and fussed because the sheriff was taking it.

"Sir, there is no posted sign anywhere that says we cannot hunt," I protested to the sheriff.

He answered, "That is not good enough. Just because there is not a sign that says, 'you may not go hunting,' it doesn't mean you may go hunting. If you are going to be smart enough to carry a weapon, son, you better be smart enough to know where you may carry that weapon. You understand that?"

I said, "Yes sir, that makes it real clear and plain. Can I have my gun back?"

The landowner and the officer fussed at us for hours until I finally got my gun. When the sheriff returned my gun, he repeated that my ignorance was an unacceptable defense.

When you plead ignorance with God, He is going to point to His Bible and say, "I wrote it down for you. Why didn't you bother to look it up? If you couldn't take the time to read it, why couldn't you go to church and listen to a man who studied the Bible and has a message from Me?"

Do You Bring Problems Upon Yourself Because of Stubbornness and Pride?

Stubbornness and pride stem from believing all things center around you. Many of life's problems are the failures associated with showing off.

My ankle is numb and marred with scars because of the pride I had as a teenager from racing motorcycles. A carload of cute girls pulled up alongside of me as I traveled to the racing track. A macho motorcycle racer cannot resist the urge to show off before single, pretty girls. I let their car get a little bit ahead of me, and then I down-shifted my bike, popped the front tire up in the air, and rolled a wheelie at 40 miles per hour past their car.

I had to steal a look. I had to make sure that they noticed how gifted, talented, and cool I was. I looked back to see that they were looking at me.

And then I flipped over backward!

I landed on my pride, and every other part of my anatomy took a turn bouncing on the pavement. My ankle took the brunt; it was twisted and packed with gravel. As a man in my fifties, I still have numbness in my ankle from that day. Every time I take a sock off and feel the area where there is no sensation, I am reminded that pride brings problems. Over thirty years later, I still struggle with a problem because of a few moments of pride. I am still paying for wanting to prove that I am somebody.

Cigarettes have snared people with their addictive chemicals. People suffer with lung cancer and emphysema because in their teenage years they "proved" how mature they were. Peer pressure forced them to take a puff. No one smokes a cigarette to enhance his health. People start smoking cigarettes because they are too proud to say "no."

Alcohol abuse starts the same way as cigarettes. It is said that alcohol is an acquired taste, which means that no one initially likes alcohol. People drink alcohol because of peer pressure or because they are trying to seem more mature. The root of this sin is pride. The problems that stem from alcohol have their roots in the pride and stubbornness of refusing to say "no." Drunks say they can handle their liquor, but their liver and brain surely cannot handle it.

Do You Bring Problems Upon Yourself Because of Fear?

Fear cripples or paralyzes people; it renders them ineffective. Fear keeps people from winning souls to Christ. Fear causes people to hide in their insecurity and withdraw into the very shadows they often fear.

The dark shadowy man brought fear to me as a child. In the dusk and nighttime hours, I believed that I saw him loitering on the railroad tracks that extended across the back of our three acres. During the daylight hours, I was not afraid of the railroad tracks. My friends and I would often hop on the trains and ride for several miles. The train would trudge up a long grade at Big Creek, so it was safe to jump off at that point. We would then take the road back. Tramps were a common sight on those trains; sometimes they would jump off on or near our property. The sighting of tramps caused my friends and me to hide in the bushes and pretend to shoot them. Tramps scared me, especially when we could see their shadows in the dusk hours.

Warren and Wayne were twins who lived down the road. They were four years older than I, but we still played together.

On one particular evening when I was six, my parents asked if Warren and Wayne could come over to the house while they went out for the evening. My sister was gone, and my parents did not want me to stay by myself. Although they were only ten, the boys and their family had a great reputation in the community. Warren and Wayne came over for the evening. We had pizza and played games.

At nine o'clock we heard the noise.

Warren said, "Jack, what was that?"

I said, "You heard it, too?" Perhaps I was imagining the sound, but if two big ten-year-olds like Warren and Wayne heard it, then I knew it was legitimate.

Wayne looked to Warren and said, "What do you think that was?"

Warren suggested, "Maybe it's the dark shadowy man that we see walking along the railroad tracks."

Wayne added, "Maybe he jumped off the train and is trying to break in the house."

The twins were not teasing me; they really thought there was danger. Our imaginations kicked in, and we schemed an elaborate plan. When the dark shadowy man came to the front door, Warren was going to answer the door and say, "Don't come any further. Jack's father is cleaning his guns!" If the dark shadowy man got through Warren and the door, Wayne was waiting behind the door with two glass 7-Up bottles. He was going to knock the dark shadowy man in the head with the bottles. Should the bottles fail, I sat under the kitchen table with my father's rifle pointed at the door and a box of ammo on the chair next to me. My job was to shoot the dark shadowy man if he made it past Warren and Wayne.

We rehearsed our plan a number of times, but we were caught off guard when the door actually burst open. Warren forgot what he was supposed to say and staggered backwards. Wayne raised the bottles in the air. I reached for my ammo.

Warren then said, "Hello, Mr. and Mrs. Schaap."

Dad looked at Wayne who had stepped out from behind the door with the raised bottles. He then looked at me under the table with the rifle. Dad failed to see any humor in our plan. He didn't understand the reason. He didn't see the genius of it all.

Dad looked at Warren and Wayne and said, "Boys, I think your mom and dad want you home right now."

They each replied with a "Yes, sir." Wayne put the bottles down, and the twins sheepishly walked out.

"What do you think you're doing?" Dad asked as he walked up to the kitchen table while I still clutched the gun.

"I am ready to shoot the dark shadowy man when he bursts in to scare us."

Dad replied, "You had better be scared of me. Give me the rifle."

Before the evening was over, Dad lectured me. He said, "Look what your fear has done. You created an imaginary person that does not exist, and you made a big scheme to conquer this imaginary enemy that is not real. Number one, it was stupid. Number two, it was a waste of time. Number three, you could have hurt somebody. Number four, you could have messed up your entire life if this went bad. Don't touch my rifle unless I give you permission and I am with you." I never forgot that incident.

Problems are self-induced when you fill your mind with the imaginary enemy. You might have shadows and bumps in the night that still haunt you today. They are immaterial. They are fears. You have concocted boogeymen. You have asked yourself, "When will this tragedy happen? When is the dark shadowy man going to enter?"

Fears are caused by the hurts and heartaches of the past. Fears are awakened by the sins of your younger years. Perhaps you are imprisoned by a fear of loving and being loved because your heart was once broken, and you refuse to have it happen again. God has given you a love that can conquer the spirit of fear, but you allow fear to control your life through the "what-if" questions. When you disable yourself because of what-ifs, you miss other pleasures. If you refuse to love because you were once hurt, you will miss the joys of loving and being loved.

You might have a real tragedy from your childhood. An incident from previous decades has paralyzed many lives. Fear puts people in a survival mode to endure each day. The fearful have dismissed their Christianity, forgetting how to live a victorious Christian life.

Fear will keep you from reaching your potential. Jesus will want to know why you hid your gifts under a bushel. He will want to know why you didn't let your light shine. Jesus will want to know who could be against you if He is for you. If fear controls your life, you won't have an answer for Christ. You will feel like my friend Wayne who realized the foolishness of his fears as he was ready to whack my dad across the head with a soda bottle.

Reflecting on Your Position

Are you ignorant about your problems? Do you know what the Bible says about your problems? Do you know your Biblical roles in your God-ordained relationships? Do you know what the Bible says about your financial practices?

Have you consulted the experts of this world on your problems? Are you ignorant about your marriage and family when you could simply read a book and get a good idea? Have you consulted the

Internet and the library about your health problem so that you can properly converse with and understand your doctors?

Where has pride brought you? Are your prideful decisions destroying your masculinity or femininity? Are they destroying your family? Before you point a finger at anyone else—including Satan—have you considered whether your pride has caused your problems?

What are your fears? Is fear paralyzing your Christian life? Has it put you in a survival mode, where you hope to endure each day? Have you forgotten to live on the victory side? Has fear caused you to dismiss the Christian life?

Advice to the Christian Engaged in Spiritual Warfare

Learn what the Bible says about your problem. Invest in a good computer program that has a concordance and commentaries. Study and meditate on references found in *Torrey's Topical Textbook*, or *The Treasury of Scripture Knowledge*. You might only need to apply one spiritual truth to conquer your problem.

Become an expert on your problem. If you struggle with finances, read books on finances and listen to radio shows about the subject. Do the same with health problems. The Internet has lots of information about diseases and medicines. Talk to people who know about your problem. You might find the one piece of advice that wins the battle.

Memorize, meditate on, and repeat Scriptures that dispel fears. Spiritual warfare uses the Bible as a sword that confronts the imaginary enemies concocted by your fears. II Timothy 1:7 says, *"For God hath not given us the spirit of fear; but of power, and of love, and of a sound mind."* Fear is as powerful as you make it because it doesn't come from God. You decide to emphasize your fears. You decide to conquer them with God's power, with love, and with your sound mind. Every time fear grips you, remind yourself that "...*God hath not given us the spirit of fear; but of power, and of love, and of a sound mind.*"

Ephesians 3:20-21 says, "*Now unto him that is able to do exceeding abundantly above all that we ask or think, according to the power that worketh in us, Unto him be glory in the church by Christ Jesus throughout all ages, world without end. Amen.*" Where is the fear in that verse?

"*I can do all things through Christ which strengtheneth me.*" Where is the fear in that verse?

"*Being confident of this very thing, that he which hath begun a good work in you will perform it until the day of Jesus Christ.*" Where does the Bible say you should have fear? Besides the fear of the Lord, the Christian is not commanded to have a fear. You are equipped to have victory.

Chapter Seven

Is God Sending You a Problem?

God could be the source of your problems. The book of Job clearly states that God gave Satan permission to test Job. People shake their fists at God because He brings problems into their lives. The fingers pointed at God might be pointed in the right direction, but those who point the fingers fail to understand why God brings those problems. If they could comprehend why God brings those problems, they would grow from the problems and not have to repeat them.

One of the greatest Biblical insights on the problems that God brings to us was made by a man who was probably unsaved. His name was Gamaliel, and he was a great Jewish scholar. Today he would be the resident expert on the faculty of an Ivy League school. Then he was a member of the Sanhedrin, which is equivalent in power to a combination of the Congress and the Supreme Court. These lawyers explained the Jewish law and created new statutes.

Members of the Sanhedrin had the power to bring a sentence upon a man, including the power of execution.

As the Sanhedrin debated how to reduce the growth of Christianity, Gamaliel offered a bit of wisdom. Some in the Sanhedrin wanted to imprison or stone the Christians because they were a theological menace to the Jewish system. Gamaliel warned his fellow lawyers not to fight against God. He gave several instances of men who rose up against Judaism but faltered after a short time. If Christianity were merely the work of men, then the new religious fad would burn out, Gamaliel warned. But if Christianity were of God, he said, *"...ye cannot overthrow it; lest haply ye be found even to fight against God."* (Acts 5:39)

The Sanhedrin faced a spiritual battle as they defended their faith. You and I would feel that their faith was misguided or misplaced, but these men believed they were fighting heresy. Gamaliel pointed out that these lawyers did not know the source of their conflict. Many of the Sanhedrin thought their conflict was with other men or the devil; few thought that it was because of themselves. Gamaliel was wise to suggest that the source of their problem just might be from God.

Many spiritual battles are the result of resisting and fighting against the Spirit of God. God brings problems into a person's life, and the person must discern when he is vainly fighting against God. People who resist God will always lose. Even Gamaliel knew that.

God Sends You Problems to Test or Increase Your Faith.

God wants you to trust Him more than you do today. Without faith it is impossible to please God, and God wants you to please Him. God wants you to relate to Him and communicate with Him and fellowship with Him. Tests increase our awareness of our need for Him.

Abraham was a man of great faith. He trusted God enough to leave his home for a new land. He trusted God when he and Sarah still did not have a baby after 99 years. God rarely had to look at Abraham and say, "Why don't you trust Me?" The Old Testament is filled with stories of how men trusted or didn't trust God. Job displayed the level of faith that God expects from his children when he said, *"Though he slay me, yet will I trust in him."* (Job 13:15a)

The biggest battle people face is putting their confidence in God. If they were confident in God, they would not struggle with Satan and this world. People wake up low on faith each day. They do not face this world confident that God will lead them. People fill their lives with addictions to escape from the dire world. Much of life is spent proving to God and this world that we don't want Him. The average Christian sees God as a good luck charm or a genie that grants three wishes. God has no interest in occupying a space amongst the gods of your world.

The problems where God is testing your faith are tests that show you how much you need God. Your Creator wants to know if He is the leader of your life. How easily Christians forget that God gives you the heartbeat, lungs, and air to sustain every moment of your life.

God Sends You Problems to Provoke You to Grow Up.

The Greek word for *provoke* describes "a sudden emotional outburst ranging from wrath to laughter." Problems may seem like an emotional outburst from God, but they are sent to mature Christians. While God wants Christians to grow up, He instead watches them cry and be filled with self-pity. People react wrongly to God's problems when they wrongly handle the Christian life, a disease, their marriage, or their children. God wants people to pull up their bootstraps and rise to the occasion. God wants to develop Christian maturity in His believers.

When I was 11 years old, my father purchased 14 acres of property that he was developing into a housing area. He decided that he and I would do as much of the construction as we could, and he would only hire other professionals as needed. When it was time to install pipe, my father hired a man with a backhoe to dig the eight-foot-deep and 660-foot-long ditch, and he hired several plumbers to physically lay the pipe. As the backhoe removed the earth, I was supposed to drop three feet of sand, the plumbers would then lay the pipe, and I would then go back and cover the pipe with three more feet of sand. The entire process was fast and furious.

Just before we did the project, a heavy rain came through our town turning the ground into a muddy clay. When the project started, I could not get traction in the tractor. All of the weight was in the front, and I couldn't do anything but spin the tires in the slop.

The digger was far ahead of me. The plumbers were waiting for me to drop the sand, so my father was paying them to stand around. Dad was down in the ditch yelling, "Son, get some sand in this ditch!" I couldn't get the tractor to move forward or backward. Dad yelled, "Get that tractor here right now!" I started crying.

Dad shouted instructions on how to pick up the sand, move the tractor in the slop, and dump the sand into the ditch. I still couldn't move the tractor. The plumbers were big bruisers, and they were laughing at me. Dad yelled more. "You are holding up everything!"

Tears streamed down my face, and I whimpered, "Dad, I can't."

Dad said, "If you are not man enough, I will get your sister."

That hurt. She was five years older than me, and she was a tough girl. I have seen my sister take a 100-pound feed sack right up on her back along with two buckets of water and walk a quarter mile to take care of a horse. She got in the tractor and gave me a proud stare that said, "I'm going to show you up." She couldn't move the tractor either. Dad yelled at her. My sister cried, and I continued crying.

Dad barked out orders. "Shut up and stop your crying. Get a shovel and start carrying buckets of sand over here."

The next morning Dad was working by 6:00 a.m., showing me how to move the tractor in the muck and how to properly deposit the sand. Dad said, "Get in that ditch and smooth it out, or I will do it myself." He thumped me on the chest with his big farmer's hands. He said, "If you want to be a man, you get on that machine, and you do it. I just showed you how to do it, now you do it. And don't you cry."

I was angry that I couldn't do it. I prayed that God would enable me. I shoved the tractor into third gear, gritted my teeth, and willed that tractor toward the ditch. I used a little too much will because I drove the tractor into the ditch. Dad wasn't angry. He hooked the tractor to a truck and pulled me out. He said, "It's about time you got some meanness in you."

All day long I was mad, but I kept dropping the sand. The plumbers were laughing at me and provoking me saying, "Come on, show your dad." I dropped a lot of sand that day.

The next year we dug many ditches and laid pipe in them. I remember my dad talking to one of the workers and saying, "No one drives the tractor like my boy does. He even beats me on it. He's the best tractor driver in the whole town." I felt 17 feet tall. I could have whipped Goliath.

My father provoked me to be better. Your Father is trying to provoke you to be better. God wants to provoke you to grow up. Your warfare might be equivalent to His yelling, "What's wrong with you? What kind of a man or woman do you call yourself?" Your warfare might be the basic training that God is using to prepare you for life.

God Sends You Problems to Chastise and Punish.

Boarding horses was another business of my father's. Our family would feed the horses, clean the stalls, and groom the horses. My job was to clean out the stalls.

Cleaning the stalls was rough in the winter. The mixture of dirty straw and manure was often frozen, so I had to break it up with a pick ax. I concocted a scheme to reduce my time in the barn. I started placing new straw over the old straw. Since the horses would just get the new straw dirty and stomp down all of the straw, I knew my Dad wouldn't notice.

The plan worked great for about a month. Day after day I would throw down fresh straw and spread it out. The horses did their jobs and stomped on it. After that first month, my Dad inspected the job I was doing.

Dad ran into the house and said, "Jack, get out to the barn right now!"

"Are the horses loose?" I asked.

"No. They're a foot taller than they were last month."

Dad led me to the barn by my ear. I had to clean out all of the dirty straw in the barn. The straw was frozen together, so I used a pick ax to break it up. I worked in the freezing cold for hours to undo my stupidity.

"He that covereth his sins shall not prosper." (Proverbs 28:13a) God sees the silly little things we do; He is not blind. We think that we can sin in the shadows, but God is light. He sees the material

things, and He sees our hearts and thoughts. Our heart is deceitful; we don't know the depths of its depravity. God says that He tries our hearts. *"The heart is deceitful above all things, and desperately wicked: who can know it? I the Lord search the heart, I try the reins...."* (Jeremiah 17:9, 10)

We think that we can cover over the problems of the heart by throwing some straw on top. That straw is made up of our good deeds, our imaginations, and our schemes to cover things up. We would like to think that God doesn't see the pile of manure growing taller and taller, just as I never thought my dad would notice the difference in the barn. God notices, and He is going to make us clean up the messes that we attempt to cover.

God sees what is underneath your straw pile, and He is going to show it to you. He might have to grab you by the ear and carry you out to the barn. He is going to hand out a pick ax and pitchfork and tell you to take care of your sins. God might be breaking your bad habit or retraining you because you do not follow His commands.

Reflecting on Your Position

Is God trying to build your faith through your problems? Is the problem in your life brought by God so that He can perfect your life and do something very spiritual in your life? Is He provoking you to grow up? Do you have straw on top of your sin? Is your problem God's way to show you what is under your straw?

Do you wake up low on faith? Do you find that your confidence in God is lacking? As you lay down to sleep, do you ever realize how few times you expressed your faith to God throughout the day? Do you face the world with God leading the way? Do you express to God your confidence in Him?

ADVICE FOR THE CHRISTIAN ENGAGED IN SPIRITUAL WARFARE

Take the time to discern the source of your problem. Be a careful Christian. Do not flippantly overreact to problems. Your first reaction to a problem should be to wonder if you brought it on yourself or if God is providing you with a lesson. You should respond properly to problems because God might make you repeat them until you learn the lesson associated with the problem.

Deal with problems that arise. If you have been caught in a sin, it is a good thing. God only bothers to catch people when He believes it will correct the problem. If you are getting by with a problem, it is because God knows you are too calloused to care. I would be scared if that were my situation.

The first step in dealing with a problem is to confess. David confessed that he was an adulterer when confronted by Nathan. His first reaction was not an excuse; it was, "I have sinned against the Lord."

Increase your faith in God's direction for your life. People who think they know what is best for their lives often find themselves in opposition to what God knows is best. God brings problems because He knows your future. He knows that you will not shine as a Christian when you are standing on a covered pile of manure. God is going to make you pitch the sin and haul it away because He loves you.

Chapter Eight

Spiritual Warfare With Yourself

Inside of every person there is a battle of spiritual warfare. It is a battle with words of how you describe yourself. Everyone has parts of himself that he does not like. Everybody wars between the old man and the new nature. Paul said in Romans 7:21-23, *"I find then a law, that, when I would do good, evil is present with me. For I delight in the law of God after the inward man: But I see another law in my members, warring against the law of my mind, and bringing me into captivity to the law of sin which is in my members."* Paul is speaking of the fight to do good while there is a spiritual war against his mind and thoughts.

Inside of me is an evil person. Every time I want to do good, the evil man accompanies me. As a pastor, I am trying to lead men and women to Christ. I am working to edify the saints and build them up spiritually, morally and ethically. I am trying to provide practical help to get them out of debt or to get a good job. I want to instill in my congregation a good work ethic, honesty, and integrity. Despite all of the good I try to do for Christ's sake, evil is present with me. I am a saved man, but I struggle with evil.

You are a saved person who still finds wretchedness in your sainthood. The Bible no longer calls you a "sinner," but sin is still present. It's as though there is another man who is accompanying you. He always disagrees with righteousness. He is always looking over your shoulder. He is your adversary. He is the wretched man. But that wretched man is as much you as is the redeemed man inside of you. He will be there until you die. You are spiritually schizophrenic. And so am I.

You want to climb spiritual peaks and stay there. You want to leave the wretched man behind. There are grand plans to dream and do, but the wretched man disapproves. Even when you climb the mountain, he is there. You huff and puff your way to the top, and he seems to have expended no energy to arrive at the same destination. He glares at you. You can read his thoughts. He is saying, "Why bother trying?"

People think that life would be better if they could only be another person. If they could only be like another person, then they wouldn't have their problems. Everybody has problems with the wretched man. No one is immune. No one's life would be better if he could be someone else.

People who don't struggle with this problem are not trying to do good. The book of Romans says that when I do good evil is present. If you aren't trying to be righteous, then you won't have a fight.

Illustrating Spiritual Warfare With Yourself

Brother Hyles, my predecessor, often told the story of God's burdening his heart to start Hyles-Anderson College. He expressed his burden to the deacons, and on the same night they voted unanimously to start the college. The thought of starting a college pumped up Brother Hyles. He was flying high as he drove home that night with a big smile and eager heart.

Someone was in the car with Brother Hyles. It wasn't a thief in the backseat. It was the wretched man. His unwanted voice said, "So you're going to start a college?"

Brother Hyles said, "That's right."

"How many faculty members do you have?" the wretched man asked.

"None, but…"

"How many buildings do you have? Do you even have a classroom?"

Brother Hyles didn't answer.

"How many students do you have?"

"None."

"How much money do you have to start the college?"

Brother Hyles winced. "None."

"You are going to start a college with no money, no buildings, no students, no faculty, and no staff?"

Brother Hyles said that he pulled over on Greenwood Avenue, got out of the car, went around the front, and opened the passenger's door. He told the wretched man, "Get out! Get out!"

I don't know if the wretched man left Brother Hyles. Every time I tell the wretched man to leave, he replies, "I can't. I'm you. You are stuck with me until you die."

The defense in spiritual warfare is fought on two simultaneous fronts. You fight the kingdom of darkness from without, while fighting the wretched man within who was once sold unto sin. It is an incredible pressure that questions your faith, your integrity, your motives, and your morality. The wretched man questions why you ever got into Christianity and why you remain devoted to it. It's not the voice from the bottomless pit; it's the voice from within. You are your own worst enemy because you can defer to the wretched man.

Reflecting on Your Position

How does the wretched man chide you? What does the wretched man keep you from accomplishing for God? Are you even in opposition to the wretched man? If not, is it because you don't try to be righteous?

ADVICE FOR THE CHRISTIAN ENGAGED IN SPIRITUAL WARFARE

Expect the presence of evil in your life. Evil is a scriptural fact.

Put off the old man. The Bible says you have to put off the old man and put on the new man. Putting off the old man is not as simple as taking off a garment. I don't think you can get rid of the old man any more than Brother Hyles could open the door and get his old nature out of him.

Putting off the old man means that you will think about what the wretched man is saying later. You are delaying it. Whatever the wretched man says, you respond by saying, "I'll do that later." You should treat the wretched man like a teenager treats his chores. Just say, "I'll get to that eventually," with no intention of getting it done. Just stall the wretched man, put him off.

Expect the wretched man to get stronger as you get older. The repetitive attacks of the wretched man are the desperate death throes of a dying nature. As you get older, the wretched man has less time to act, so he must act more severe. Battles get harder as you get older. The most difficult warfare that I conduct is now. I expect it to be harder in ten years. I am growing as a Christian, but the wretched man grows more vile.

When I was five, my greatest evil was stealing a cookie. As I grow older, the wretched man is more cunning, slippery, disgusting, vulgar, ungodly, and unChristian. He becomes all the more dastardly, devious, defiling, depraved, disgusting, and deceitful.

When I die, I will leave the wretched man behind. I will be with Jesus and have a new body free from the wretched man. But for now those two natures are in a battle.

Your desire to be delivered will increase as you age. Young people believe they will conquer the world. Old people look at the young and say, "Just hope you are standing when the battle is done."

God's grace will enable you to stand. The spotlight of God's grace will empower. Once you find that you cannot succeed against the wretched man, you learn a lesson in humility. It is then that God looks to you.

Job humbled himself. He said, *"Wherefore I abhor myself, and repent in dust and ashes."* After he humbled himself, Job was blessed with God's grace. He received twice as many possessions as he previously possessed.

When a person has been beaten by the wretched man, he won't be inspired. As a pastor I have tried to re-inspire people to continue. They say, "You haven't been kicked in the teeth, have you? You didn't climb the mountain just to have your hand stepped on and squashed when you grasped for the top." When people get their fingers squished and teeth kicked in, they don't want to try anymore. Some people won't be inspired, but they need to humbly let God pick them up.

Don't confuse hurting with humility. Job was hurting throughout the book of Job, but he wasn't humble until the last chapter. Job repented of believing that he could impress God and work his way out of the mess. He repented of believing that he could show God how diligent and faithful and worthy he was of God's blessing. God waited for Job to realize His faithfulness. That was the humility that God sought.

God is not most interested in **great Christians** with faith in God. God is not most interested in Christians with **great faith** in God. God is most interested in Christians with faith in a **great God.**

If you are not careful, you will think that you need to prove your greatness to God. Christians try to prove that they were worthy of saving. Christians were saved to show that God is worthy of being bragged about.

Grace will lift you when you lower yourself to be humble. God will allow you to sink to the bottom with squished fingers and broken teeth until you say, "Forgive me for trying to show You how good I am. I have discovered that I am not very good. I have nothing to offer You."

Chapter 9

Spiritual Warfare Against My Feelings

Satan is successful in spiritual warfare when he confuses facts and feelings. His campaign against the Gospel has confused the truth of salvation with people's feelings on how they can be saved. The majority of humans do not know how to get to Heaven. Satan is successful when people believe they don't need the truth because they feel that they are good enough for Heaven or they feel that all roads lead to the same place. The Prince of Darkness is very successful at blinding the minds of people to the truth and simplicity of the Gospel.

The damages of spiritual warfare are not only calculated by the number of unsaved people. Satan has used feelings to sidetrack and derail Christians. Saved Christians have the Spirit of God living in them which gives them the potential to be as Spirit-filled as Christ was. It makes little sense that Christians live defeated when they have the promises of God in the Bible. The Scriptures are filled with examples of saints who suffered affliction with a good attitude. The Word of God teaches that there is victory in the end.

However, Christians habitually backslide and struggle. Many Christians find that their lives are tedious; they are boring and endured. The victorious Christian life seems as mythical to some as the pot of gold at the end of the rainbow. It makes no sense for saved people to have a poor spirit when God travels with them. Yet so many Christians have a fallen countenance. Why should the journey be so dour?

Satan's ultimate destiny is defeat and punishment, yet Christians allow him much access. Feelings are the easiest way that Satan can access your spirit and gain an advantage on you. Satan wants you to trust your feelings as the most reliable source of truth. He wants you to focus on your feelings rather than the truth. He knows that feelings are more real than the truth is to most people. He knows that people interpret a situation by how they feel about a matter.

All feelings ultimately find their origin in our thoughts. Therefore, this struggle is a spiritual battle over words. Satan has discovered that man is an emotional creature who is naturally responsive to feelings before truth. Satan counterbalances truth by repeating lies until your emotions succumb. He creates an unstable Christian.

Don't let your feelings determine truthfulness instead of letting the truth transform your feelings. One will always influence the other. Feelings become the perceived truth when you elevate and react to your emotional stimuli.

The divorce rate is high because people don't feel the love for their spouse anymore. They do not confront their feelings with the truth that what "...God hath joined together, let not man put asunder."

Candidates are chosen based on how voters feel about an image instead of the truth of a voting record. How I feel about abortion should be irrelevant when compared to God's truth of when life begins. Jeremiah 1:5 says, *"Before I formed thee in the belly I knew thee; and before thou camest forth out of the womb I sanctified thee, and I ordained thee a prophet unto the nations."* God told Jeremiah that He knew him before conception.

Some of the arguments for abortion are compelling because they tug at people's feelings. Poor girls are taken advantage of, abused, and violated. Young ladies who are trying to get out of the slums and ghettos find they are pregnant and worry that they won't get their feet on solid ground. There is nothing wrong with empathizing, but everyone must decide if feelings will trump the truth.

Abortion is not the issue here, but it is a good example of how people choose feelings over facts. The same could be applied to marriage, education, child rearing, church building, and money. Many Christians feel that they can't make it if they tithe, yet tithing is commanded in the Bible.

Standing with the truth is scary. Hebrews 11 says that people who stood for truth got their heads cut off, were cut in pieces with a saw, were thrown to the lions, were persecuted by satanic oppression, and were prosecuted and persecuted by governments. Standing with the truth is a scary place because it is a foreign location to many. However, the truth is a stable place because it is where God resides.

The Security of Your Feelings

People find security in their feelings because they have built their life around feelings. Opinions and emotions are governed by feelings. "That's just the way I feel" has become an excuse to ignore the truth.

People do not opt for the truth because they do not find security in God. Faith is equated to losing control and placing God in control. Since people can choose their feelings, they find security in that which they control. Your challenge is to find your security in God so that your feelings do not control your decisions.

Reflecting on Your Position

Do you base your life on truth or feelings? Do feelings or truth prevail when they are in opposition? On what do you base the truth that forms your opinions?

ADVICE FOR THE CHRISTIAN ENGAGED IN SPIRITUAL WARFARE

Philippians 4 explains how to put our feelings under the control of the truth. Christians trust their feelings when they do not feel secure with God. God promises that if we obtain the peace of God, we will have a sound heart and mind. Philippians 4:7 says, *"And the peace of God, which passeth all understanding, shall keep your hearts and minds through Christ Jesus." Keep* means "to guard." The guard is the peace of God, a tool that helps people who are living on their feelings.

The initial objective is to find the peace of God, although the peace of God is not the endgame. The ultimate purpose in finding the peace of God is to find the God of peace, as stated in Philippians 4:9. The pursuit of God is vital in battling spiritual warfare. Don't desire the insulation of His peace without wanting the presence of God. Don't desire the narcotic of peace to dull your senses from the pain of your circumstances, but never pursue God. If you pursue God, you will find more than a temporary narcotic. You will find *"fulness of joy…[and]…pleasures for evermore."* (Psalm 16:11) The following steps will help you to find the peace of God and the God of peace.

"Rejoice in the Lord...." **(Philippians 4:4)** *Rejoice* means "to enjoy once again." This verse specifically says to enjoy God the way you once enjoyed Him. Enjoy God the way you did when you first got saved. Look at God the way you did when the sermons moved your heart and you made decisions for Him that you knew would impact your life. Enjoy Him the way you did when tears would run down your face as you sang a certain song or heard a certain sermon. Enjoy something about the Lord that you once immensely enjoyed.

Some Christians never enjoyed the Lord, so they have never had peace. They fret, worry, and mumble. They are confused, disturbed, distracted, and depressed because they have yet to enjoy the Lord. It is hard to enjoy again what you never enjoyed in the first place.

Is there a song about the Lord that you enjoy? Is there a passage of Scripture that particularly excites you and thrills your heart? Don't let a Bible reading schedule keep you from enjoying your favorite passages of Scripture. Read the portions that excite you. Is there a book in the Bible in which you revel? Is there a sermon that brought you a little closer to Heaven? Is there one that stirs your passion to do great things for God?

Victory over your emotions starts by getting excited about the unchanging God of truth. Circumstances don't bring stability because they change. Paul wrote this letter from a jail cell. He had poor circumstances, but he had stability in the presence of God. The presence of your Father should be your security and peace. If your emotions trump truth, then you do not find the security of your Father's presence. That is why you need to remind yourself of the times when you found great joy in Him.

"Let your moderation be known unto all men." **(Philippians 4:5a)** *Moderation* is "modesty." It is also "meekness,

humility, kindness, respect, or propriety." A moderate man has self-control and is reasonable. Meek people treat all people as equals. A moderate man understands that everyone can have a different opinion. He doesn't make snap judgments. The truth that God loves another as much as He loves him trumps his feelings about someone's religion, race, or age.

Too many people deflate others to comparatively pump up themselves. When you let your moderation be known unto all men, you accept your place in life even if it means someone appears better. You do not exalt how wonderful you are. When you let other people win, you are the victor to Christ.

Feelings are determined by whether or not we think we are superior to someone else. People feel good to the degree that they are better, higher, smarter, or wiser than another. People feel down when they see that someone has a leg up on them. Feelings vacillate up and down as someone evaluates himself in comparison to another. Such a person is emotionally driven.

The person who is truth driven becomes a servant and finds emotional stability. He says to the man on top, "Congratulations! You have earned it." He exalts the man of low degree and says, "God bless you."

The man of moderation is strong enough to yield to everyone. He lets the rusty Yugo or the Escalade cut into traffic ahead of him because he is not a respecter of persons. He puts his feelings in the backseat and finds emotional stability because he is not subject to the highs and lows of searching for superiority.

"Be careful for nothing." (Philippians 4:6a) *Careful* means "to be full of care or to be anxious or nervous." *Careful* is how you feel about the circumstances of life. God is essentially saying that you should not let your feelings determine your response and actions. Feelings should not alter or bend your life. God wants you

to talk to Him about your feelings so that you do not get bent out of shape or infect others with a bad spirit.

"In every thing by prayer and supplication with thanksgiving let your requests be made known unto God." **(Philippians 4:6b)** God doesn't mind if you vent to Him. Prayer is an act of faith that shows God you desire His involvement. There are three specific things that you can do to avoid getting bent out of shape: (1) tell God what you want Him to do; (2) supplicate; (3) be thankful.

Tell God what you want Him to do. There is nothing wrong with giving God your thoughts and feelings and opinions on a matter, but prayer doesn't inform God; He is omniscient. You can tell God what you think about your circumstances, but prayer is not simply venting your emotions. Prayer is asking God to give divine involvement.

Don't exclude God. Some people are afraid to pray because they don't want to be denied by God. They would rather have their way than have His perfect will. The joy of God's will trumps what you can imagine.

Supplicate. When you are anxious, God wants to hear intense, fervent prayer. *"The effectual fervent prayer of a righteous man availeth much."* (James 5:16b) Supplication values God's opinion even if it is different than yours. Supplication wants to hear God's opinion. Supplication pleads for God's will to be done.

Give thanks. When you are anxious, thank God for what is making you anxious. Give thanks for everything He does. Thank God for what He is doing and for how He will use this for His glory. Whether you get your way or not, thank God because He is sovereign and His opinion overrules yours. You can give thanks for all things because you know that God is in charge. What a peaceful thought! Peace comes when you can rest in the perfect will of God.

"Those things, which ye have both learned, and received, and heard, and seen in me, do: and the God of peace shall be with you." **(Philippians 4:9)** God has given us an example of perfected Christians. Paul demonstrated to the Philippians how to handle bad circumstances. Today we have our own saints among us who have handled crises. These people serve as our examples. The Philippians were to ask, "What would Paul do?" We can ask, "What would my friend who has gone through the fire do?"

You need to follow a godly person who has been stable during the tough times. He will help to keep you stable. Develop a group of advisors who can warn you of the troubles to come. Consult them when you don't know what to do. Familiarize yourself with the biographies of good Christians and learn how they triumphed. Study the accounts in the Bible of people who overcame worse situations than you.

You have the mind of God when you have these layers of protection. When you implement these ingredients, you can have the confidence that you know the truth and how you should feel. The presence of God is peace. There is no fretting or worrying; it is just a calm assurance. God says that when you add these six ingredients to your life, you will have His presence. Thus, you can be assured that you are following the correct path.

Section Four

THE BATTLE PLAN

Chapter Ten

The Generational Warrior

Satan's greatest offensive front is against your family. God first placed a family and not a church in the Garden of Eden. If Satan can break up the family, then he can break up the church. If he can break up a family, he can divide people from God. Destroying a family is the first domino that can knock over the other God-ordained relationships.

The Psalmist of Psalm 106 said, *"We have sinned with our fathers, we have committed iniquity, we have done wickedly."* When the Bible mentions fathers, the meaning is not restricted to a biological father. It refers to the previous generations. The psalmist said that certain sins were committed by his great-great-grandfathers, great-grandfathers, grandfathers, and father. He confessed that he had the same sins.

If you traced your lineage back a few generations, you would probably notice a habitual weakness in your family. There are sins that visit each generation. Most generations submit to the sin and injure their potential.

Iniquity is the permission we give ourselves to sin. Satan has built a castle in our soul that houses our sinful nature. Our iniquity is a stronghold. The iniquity toward specific sins seems to become a part of our DNA that is passed on to successive generations.

The inheritance of fathers is not just cars, houses, and money. The inheritance includes the iniquities of the fathers. Children are born addicted to alcohol. Some are pickled in the womb and end up distorted or unstable. Pregnant teenagers often give birth to children who become pregnant teenagers. All of this happens because Mom and Dad passed down a nature that physically decimated the child before he drew his first breath. The generational sin might be infidelity to the church. Grandpa left church, Dad left church, and now the son is out of church. Improper financial stewardship might plague your family. These are all generational sins.

You might have been molested as a child by someone in your family who was molested when they were a child. If you looked into it, you might find that molestation goes back many generations. Each successive generation was infected by the sins of the fathers. Victims of molestation have told me that they are scared the same thing will happen to their children.

Adultery and divorce taint the bloodlines of many families. Relatives have been married two and three and four or more times. People in your family might get married and have no desire to stay married. They might have an affair and have no concern for the wedding vows. Maybe no one in your family gets married for keeps. Maybe it is part of your family. Maybe it's the generational sin.

Successive generations receive a spiritual fingerprint of sin. They are born in the battle of spiritual warfare. The devil and his horde already know what the weaknesses are in the family. They know where to start the temptation of the new generation.

Despite the inevitability of the sin visiting each generation,

God prepares generational warriors. They are the people who have escaped the sin once it visited them. God raises up generational warriors who sense the problem and desire to fix it.

Who Is the Generational Warrior?

I define a generational warrior as one who defends the future generations from the satanic opposition that has felled the previous generations. The generational warrior wants to battle the sins that have besieged his soul and have besieged the lives of his family and fellow human beings. God raises up a generational warrior in every family, generation, church, and society. God ordains warriors for denominations and for governments. The generational warrior has been given grace by God. He has received extra strength to wield his sword and defend with his shield so that he can bring deliverance to his time.

God searches each generation for the people who have the right heart. II Chronicles 16:9 says, *"For the eyes of the Lord run to and fro throughout the whole earth, to shew himself strong in the behalf of them whose heart is perfect toward him...."* God is constantly searching the heart of man for someone whose heart is sensitive to Him. Those whose hearts are not in tune with God have war. Perhaps God has to search the whole earth because there is only a handful of people who have sensitive hearts. Those whose hearts are in tune with God have the potential to be generational warriors.

Perhaps you have been chosen to be a generational warrior. Perhaps God has already delivered you from some of the bondage that enslaves your family. You might be an aberration in your family. Family members might view your relationship with God as a foreign religion. Perhaps some family members won't even speak to you because of your stand for God. They might be in a very different religion or environment. They are in bondage to the same addictions that once fettered you. The grace of God lifted you out of the miry clay. God's grace brought you face to face with the truth that quickened you and made sense. The new awareness brought a new substance to your existence. In your heart you ask yourself, "Why did I get it? How come they don't understand? Why was I chosen?"

Perhaps you are the generational warrior.

The warrior might be a little one who is going through adolescence. He might not be able to read the Bible yet, but God is working in his heart at this tender age. He might be like Samuel, the generational warrior reared in the house of Eli. Samuel grew up in the midst of vile brothers who made a mockery of the priesthood. His foster father, Eli, was a man given to gluttony and allowed his sons to be vile. God spoke to Samuel as a little boy. Samuel responded, *"Speak, Lord; for thy servant heareth."* Samuel's young heart was in tune with God.

The generational warrior might be the young person who realizes in the depth of his heart that he is not like all his buddies who behave immorally and look at things they shouldn't. For some reason he finds himself with a desire for holiness and righteousness, and he can't figure out why. There are young men throughout this world who have no idea what God has in mind, but their hearts want to hear what God is saying.

The warrior might be a teenager like David. No adult warrior— not even the king—would fight Goliath. David was mocked when he arrived at the camp of the Israelite army. His own brothers told him to go back to shepherding. David accepted the challenge of fighting Goliath. He slew the giant with a stone and cut off Goliath's head with a sword. The Philistines then fled but were chased down by the Israelites. David delivered his generation when no adult would fight.

The warrior might be a father who was God-ordained to break the sins of the family. He is a man who is determined to beat the sins that have plagued his family. He is the man who won't use his father or grandfather as an excuse to sin. He is the man who does not wait to see if his son will be a generational warrior. He decides to wage the battle on his watch.

Who Rejected Being a Generational Warrior?

Some don't respond to God's call to be a generational warrior. God raised up Samson to be a judge over Israel, but Samson couldn't leave women alone. He never seriously accepted his responsibility. The future was unaffected by Samson's life. He could have beaten the Philistines, but that was left for David to accomplish many years later. Samson did not deliver his generation.

Saul was called to be a generational warrior, but he served himself instead of his generation. Once the throne was taken from Saul, he could have prepared David to be the king. Instead, Saul hunted for David while the Philistines prepared for battles. Saul was eventually killed by the Philistines, the people whom he should have pursued when he was hunting David.

The Ultimate Battle of the Generational Warrior

When an individual decides to be a generational warrior, he must understand that the ultimate battle is not between good and evil. The ultimate battle is between pride and humility. Every generational sin is the product of pride and can be solved with a humble spirit of a man who realizes he is in the spotlight of God's grace.

Pride is the foundation for every sin. Pride is an expression of independence from God. Pride is contending for God's supremacy and His right to decide. Pride is what keeps your family in bondage.

Pride causes divorce, disrespect for authority, personal defilement, and church splits. Pride originated with Satan, the instigator of spiritual warfare. He said, "*I* will be like God. *I* will sit in His throne. *I* will be exalted unto the heavens."

If pride were properly confessed to God, you would say, "God, I have tried to demonstrate how little I care about You, how little I want You in my life, how much I want to show You I don't need You, and how I think I have the right to sit on Your throne and be my own God."

The entire life of Jesus Christ centered around what would happen at the Cross. Pride put Christ on the Cross. The humility of Christ permitted His crucifixion. The grace of God was the end result.

The pride of the generational warrior makes him think that he is doing God a favor. He might start thinking that he was pulled from the depths because he was better than others. He might think that he was chosen for his greatness. Jesus didn't scold people for wanting to be great, but he explained greatness in terms of humility and the abasement of pride. Jesus said that if you want to be great, you must first serve everyone.

The greatness and effectiveness of the generational warrior is found in his humility when he becomes a servant to all and can give his life as a ransom for their lives. In the Bible days, a ransom was what you paid for the freedom of a convicted criminal, slave, or common thug. Jesus Christ came to give Himself as a ransom for many. He knew that He was buying the freedom of the abominable. The generational warrior works so that others can be freed from the sins that enslave his family.

The generational warrior is laying down his life for the thugs, the indigent, the poor, the addicted, the incarcerated, the convicted, the worthless, the unworthy, the lowlife, the demeaned, the unpopular, the unlovely, and the unloving. Jesus was the ultimate generational warrior because He came out from among the people to help others rise out of their mess.

The generational warrior will have to deal with pride. The question is not whether or not you have any pride. The question is whether you can identify the different places where pride rears its ugly head. Even within churches, we rear a generation with pride as a tool. We teach people to be proud of who they are and to make something of themselves. The generational warrior makes something of someone else.

Reflecting on Your Position

Are you going to be a victim or a warrior? What are the generational sins of your family? What has plagued your great-grandparents, grandparents, and parents? Are the generational sins sexual in nature? Are they sins of the tongue and attitudes? Are the generational sins of alcohol and other drugs? Does the squandering of money run in your blood? How do you struggle with the same sins? How have those sins hurt you? If you are a parent, do you see those sins hurting your children or grandchildren? Where is pride keeping you from being the generational warrior?

ADVICE TO THE CHRISTIAN ENGAGED IN SPIRITUAL WARFARE

Identify the generational sins of your family. Take an honest look at the problems that have afflicted your ancestors, afflict you, and afflict your children. Take an honest look at whether or not the problems of your fathers have hurt you.

Decide if you will be a generational warrior. If you are reading this book, it is likely that you are a generational warrior. You are seeking to win the battle in spiritual warfare because your heart is in tune with God or because you are tired of consistently losing the battle. You must decide that you will not give place to Satan in your home and in your life.

The next chapter will teach you how to battle, but the decision must first be made to do battle. Samuel decided to accept what the Lord would say. David took up Goliath's offer to fight. There must be a moment where you declare that you will fight against spiritual warfare. I challenge you to pick up that Word of God and declare war. Deliver your family. Deliver your generation.

Consider the consequences if you choose not to be a generational warrior. Your children, your grandchildren, and your great-grandchildren need you to achieve victory over the sin. Just as you have been hurt by the sins of your fathers, your children will be hurt by the same sins. If you deal with generational sins now, they can fight greater battles in the future because they will not be bogged down by the generational sins.

Develop humility, and you will capture God's attention. Humility is a confession of your intense need for God. Isaiah 66:2 says, *"For all those things hath mine hand made, and all those things have been, saith the LORD: but to this man will I look, even to him that is poor and of a contrite spirit, and trembleth at my word."* The person who is *"poor and of a contrite spirit"* is a humble person. God says that He will look at the person who is humble. God focuses His spotlight of grace on the humble.

God resists the proud. If you are trying to have God fight the battle of spiritual warfare, do not have Him resist you. It is tough enough when the devil resists you. You do not want God doing the same. If you fight against God, you don't have a chance for success.

God gives grace to the humble. Grace is God's supernatural blessing. Grace is that blessing from God that tends to take the work you do and make it last forever. The generational warrior who is looking to save his home from Satan's attacks would be wise to fall on his face before God and ask for wisdom from God who ordained the home. God will focus on you His spotlight of grace when you demonstrate humility.

If you feel that God doesn't care about you or your family, increase your humility. Perhaps He truly isn't focusing His blessings in your direction because areas of your life tell Him that He is not needed. The humble have the wind of God at their backs and underneath their wings. The humble are asking God to focus His attention on them and fight for them in spiritual warfare.

Chapter Eleven

Preparing Yourself
for Warfare

The prophet Daniel was one of the great generational warriors described in the Bible. Daniel is an extreme example of a generational warrior because he did not just bring deliverance for a family. Because Daniel took a stand, he delivered himself from bondage and ultimately delivered the entire nation from bondage and changed the course of history. Daniel understood that he was wrestling with the powers of the kingdom of darkness and declared, "We are going to change the course we are taking."

The book of Daniel contains powerful truths that will bring deliverance to families and individuals and churches and societies and nations. You can learn how to change the outcome of your family's future history. You can learn how to have your family follow the Lord. You can learn to be a generational warrior by studying Daniel's example.

Daniel Accepted the Challenge of Being a Generational Warrior.

The call of God goes out to many people. Matthew 22:14 says, *"For many are called, but few are chosen."* This is a famous verse, but people are confused about its meaning. The first issue is that you must choose to listen to the call. Secondly, you must choose to be chosen. Few people who hear the call of God say, "I accept the challenge." God issues the call to many people. God has called many people to be generational warriors, but most of those allow their generational sins to plague them instead of accepting the challenge.

Choose God's calling. Understand that the problems and afflictions of your family are numerous, and you will allow God to conquer those sins through you. The calling does not make you superior to other family members. The calling does not mean that you have to distance yourself from your family. The calling means that God thinks that your heart is in tune with His heart. You should be humble when you realize that God said, "I want you!" The choosing means that you have chosen to accept the challenge.

Daniel's calling was profound. Jerusalem was besieged by the Babylonians. Many Jews were killed, but the promising young men were chosen to be trained in the arts of the Babylonians. Daniel was one of the promising young men who was shackled behind a team of camels and marched one thousand miles following the Fertile Crescent. They marched north through Syria, east through Assyria, and down into Babylon, which is modern day Iraq. The journey was four to six months. Daniel would never see home again.

People fail to answer the call to be a generational warrior because they do not succeed in the great trials of physical ailments and family troubles. People don't want to be separated from their family as Daniel was separated. People don't want to lose their security as Daniel lost his security. They fail to realize that God has chosen these trials for a purpose. They fail to realize that God will bring them through the trials. They don't consider what is on the other side of the trial as Daniel considered the potential once he got to Babylon.

People fail to accept the challenge because they worry that the challenge involves afflictions like wheelchairs and miscarriages. They are afraid of the pain they might have to endure to be used of God. Daniel will receive a lot of rewards on his judgment day, but people would rather not suffer the journey to Babylon to receive the rewards of enduring. Afflictions do not come unless a providential, sovereign Lord of the universe allows those things to happen. As He did for Moses, He lights the bush on fire to see if you will turn aside and see a great sight.

Daniel had a lot of time to think during this journey. Daniel was very resolved once he got to Babylon. He must have decided that God was in charge of this situation. He must have decided that the calamity would not be wasted. Daniel had to accept that God was bringing him through great trials for a purpose. Daniel was calculating his next move. I believe he knew that something big was going to happen once he reached Babylon.

Daniel Realized in His Heart That There Was a Purpose for the Afflictions.

You have to realize there is a purpose for the affliction caused by generational sins. God spared you for a reason. The greatest reason is that God has a divine message that your life teaches your family. The message is not, "I'm not like you anymore," because then the purpose would be all about you. The message is about a gracious God.

The destination of being a generational warrior is humility. The obstacle is pride. The rewards are grace. God has chosen you to display His grace to your family. The generational warrior says, "By the grace of God, I was delivered from that sin. Now I want to deliver my family."

The Bible says that *"...Daniel purposed in his heart that he would not defile himself..."* once he came to Babylon. The end result of understanding he had a purpose was the promotion of Daniel to glorify God in the heathen kingdom of the Babylonians.

Daniel Identified the Enemy.

You cannot be a generational warrior if you do not know the enemy. You must identify the besetting sin of the previous generations. You will dabble in being a generational warrior if you do not identify the exact sin that has beset your generations.

Daniel 9 contains a prayer of confession and pleading by Daniel. He confessed the sins of his nation. He said that Israel was guilty of departing from God's precepts and judgments. Daniel confessed that they had not listened to the prophets who spoke on God's behalf. Daniel told God that Israel had become a reproach because of their sins and because of the iniquities of the fathers. He was essentially telling God that Israel had generational sins of rebellion against God and a disregard for His law. Daniel named what he was fighting against.

Reflecting on Your Position

Have you decided yet if you are a generational warrior? Have you identified the sins of your family? Will you trust God in the afflictions? Will you believe that He has a greater purpose for your problems?

ADVICE TO THE CHRISTIAN ENGAGED IN SPIRITUAL WARFARE

Don't dabble in being a generational warrior. Be committed. If you dabble, you are only wielding a plastic sword. You will be a pretender. You can claim to be a generational warrior, but you will be of no effect. Perhaps you need to say to God, "Our nation is in a most precarious situation. If you will use me, I will change history with you."

Expect to take a long time to conquer spiritual warfare. The book of Daniel spans decades of his life. He dedicated himself to war as a teenager, and he was still being used by God as an old man. Your problems will not be solved quickly. The remainder of your life might be spent as a generational warrior engaging the Devil in spiritual warfare.

Live a life that prepares for the long haul. A great man like Moses spent one third of his life preparing in the back side of the desert. The development of a generational warrior takes a long time. You will not become one because you are inspired by a chapter in a book or by a sermon.

Be honest with God about the sins of your family. Daniel was transparent about the sins of his nation. Lay those sins before God. Stop whitewashing the sins of your family, your community, and your nation. Agree with God that you and the others around you have wrong thinking. If your thinking was in step with God, you wouldn't have your problems.

Set yourself for war through prayer. Daniel is seen praying in chapters 2, 6, 9 and 10. Prayer was his passion, not his duty. God is the one who will bring the victory in spiritual warfare. Talk with Him because you are passionate about Him, not because you are obligated to Him. I don't talk to my wife because it is my duty; I talk to my wife because she is my passion. Treat God in like manner. Bear your heart and soul to Him. Ask Him for the wisdom to understand the sins that beset your generation.

Daniel confessed the sins to God. Confession is a statement to God that says you are in agreement with Him. Generational warriors are in a constant battle to align their thinking with God's thinking.

Set yourself for war through fasting. Daniel fasted from the king's meat. When he earnestly sought God in chapter 9, he did so with fasting. Fasting results in spiritual enlightenment. It puts an appetite in the heart to achieve spiritual success heretofore unseen.

A generational warrior begins the battle by diminishing his appetite for the world. Not everything that he puts away is wrong, but he puts himself in a position where he craves the things of God.

Increase your dedication to the Lord. The time you take to be holy is the best time you will take. A generational warrior sets aside chunks of time for God. He does not give God an excuse that he cannot find time for his Creator. Ignore something else from your schedule if you can't find time for God.

Take the necessary time to bring holiness to your home and to bring righteousness to the next generation. Be a warrior who goes to his knees in prayer. Be a warrior who will fast from food or the television. Skip one meal per week and dedicate an hour to praying for your family. Show God that this needed victory is more important than the other things to which you have devoted your attention.

The generational warrior is ultimately preparing his heart to serve God. The generational warrior does not know how God will use him to fight the battle, so he is sharpening all of his tools in preparation. He is preparing his heart to be ready for God's commands.

Increase your passion for the Lord. He is not a nuisance; He is your life. He is not an interference in your regularly scheduled programming. He is your program content, your director, and producer. Do not say, "I don't mind being a Christian." Love being a Christian. Meditate on the blessings He has provided, and your heart will grow warm toward Him.

Chapter Twelve

Taking Your Stand
Against Satan

The book of Ephesians compares spiritual warfare to wrestling. Success in wrestling is not directly correlated to body size, body shape, or the amount of muscle. Wrestlers win because they can think faster than their opponent, choose the correct countermove, and implement the move faster than their opponent. As a generational warrior, you need to learn the spiritual countermoves.

My physical education teacher at Pillsbury Baptist Bible College was a man named David Hazewinkel. He earned a Greco-Roman bronze medal in the 1969 world championships. One year later he took the silver. Mr. Hazewinkel represented the United States in the 1968 and 1972 Olympics. Greco-Roman wrestlers need upper body strength. Mr. Hazewinkel was huge in his upper body. He was v-cut. He was a tough teacher.

Some of the students who wrestled in gym class didn't

understand his ability. One big kid in particular always looked like he wanted to fight someone. One day in class, Mr. Hazewinkel said to the tough kid, "Do you wrestle?"

"Yeah," the tough kid replied and went to the teacher. Within two seconds, the kid was knocked on his back, gasping for air.

Mr. Hazewinkel said, "Who's next?"

No one offered to take him on. We didn't wrestle him. We stood in awe of him. He knew more wrestling moves than we did. None of us could have beaten him.

Satan knows more wrestling moves than you. He will pin you on the mat the moment the match begins. No person is a match for Satan. No one has the moves or the muscle to beat him. God gives you the wisdom to withstand and survive. Spiritual victory will ultimately be won when you allow God to fight the battle.

As a boy, my friends and I would set up wrestling rings in my father's chicken coop. It was always tag-team wrestling with my third cousin, Kelly, and two boys from down the street, Dan and Harvey. Dan was a thick boy who loved to pick on people. Harvey was over six-feet tall in junior high and skinny as a noodle. Dan and Harvey hated each other.

I was the smallest one in the group, so Dan and I always teamed up against Kelly and Harvey. Dan always had the same strategy. I would wrestle Harvey until I could lay my hand over the edge of the mat so that Dan could slap it. At that point Dan would come in the ring and thrash Harvey.

Harvey never seemed to catch on to Dan's plan. I hated wrestling Harvey, because he would kick me in the shin with his boots. Every time, however, I would navigate the fight to the side of the mat, let Dan slap my hand, and be relieved by Dan who overmatched Harvey.

God wants to be your tag-team wrestling partner. God wants

you to slap His hand so that He can come in the ring and stomp Satan. Since you cannot defeat the kingdom of darkness, you need to plug into a different power. You will not beat spiritual warfare by trying harder. If trying a little harder would make the difference, you wouldn't need God. The Christian life is not about showing God how tough you are; it is about letting God show you His toughness. Your willpower won't defeat Satan.

You fear Satan without cause. You have the omnipotent God on your side. Resist the devil, and he will flee. The devil will run when he sees that God fights for you.

The Picture of a Defeated Christian

The Christian who is defeated in spiritual warfare never allowed God to fight the battle and never used the resources that God gave him. Paul admonished the Ephesians to put on the full armor of God. Many Christians will use God when Satan has them backed into an alley. God wants to be there before you get backed into an alley. God wants to be a part of every battle in the war.

Too many Christians have assigned God to a grandstand position. They want God to be a cheerleader when they are discouraged. They want to run their own race and show God how well they can do it. God is the pit crew when they need a tire change or refueling.

This Christian will falter and stumble. His pride will get in the way of calling upon God. As he tries harder, he digs his heels deeper in the mud. He is too proud to look to the Bible. God's great tool of help is ignored. Without the Bible, he is ignorant of the combat maneuvers that would bring deliverance.

Job: The Picture of the Victor in Spiritual Warfare

Job's patience to endure affliction is remembered in James 5.

As the Devil beat him and as his friends accused him of deserving the punishment, Job said, *"Though he slay me, yet will I trust in him."* God stopped Satan from afflicting Job when Job repented, humbled himself, and prayed for his friends. Job stood with those in his God-ordained relationships—God, his wife, and his friends—and received twice what he had lost.

ADVICE TO THE CHRISTIAN ENGAGED IN SPIRITUAL WARFARE

Stand with those in your God-ordained relationships. When speaking about spiritual warfare in Ephesians 6:11-14, the Bible commands us to stand three times. Paul is not speaking to one Christian in this passage; he is speaking to an entire congregation. Paul's words give the image of soldiers standing shoulder to shoulder in their squad. There is an armor to put on, but it is not for the offensive. It is to defend off spiritual warfare while God beats the Devil.

You fight spiritual warfare to the degree you stand with those in your God-ordained relationships. When someone is having a hard time, you stand with him. When the church goes through a hard time, you stand with the people. You are insecure if you flee when trouble arises. You will gain confidence when your relationship blossoms as you stand with someone.

When you are frustrated by the afflictions and say, "I've tried everything the Bible says," remain standing. When your friends are being assaulted by the devil, extend a hand to them and say, "I'm with you."

Job's wife and friends did not stand with Job, but he ultimately decided to stand with God and with them. Job's wife said, *"Curse God, and die."* Job's friends told him why he deserved God's punishment. Job told God that he was standing with Him. Job prayed for his friends—a sign that he stood with them.

Stand with God by giving Him your confidence and trust. God provides stability and security for you to enjoy. Stand with His Bible. Give Him a life that is befitting of His holiness.

Parents need to stand with their children, and children need to stand with their parents. Stability is formed when there is trust between parents and children. No child should be given full control of his life, but he needs a parent who trusts him a little.

Stand with your spouse as you promised on the wedding day when you said, "till death do us part," and, "for better for worse."

Don't push people away. Tough times are not the times to push away. That is division; that is Satanism. You do the work for Satan when you push people away. Become familiar with saying to others, "You are going through a tough time, aren't you? We're going to figure out a way to get through this."

Don't push children away. Discipline, but don't segregate them. Children who don't find their emotional stability in Mom and Dad are going to find it in someone who will steal their heart. Parents must develop a bond of security based on relationship and not achievement.

A husband might push his wife away when she is going through physical and emotional changes. When a spouse goes through a tough time, don't push him away. When a wife is going through physical and emotional changes, the husband needs to stand by her.

Never push away anyone in your God-ordained relationships. Be the warrior of whom it could be said, "He withstood in the evil day. He kept standing."

Stop being suspicious. Don't lose your faith in humanity. Don't lose your confidence in the people you love and serve.

Job's wife and friends were suspicious. She counseled Job to curse God and die. Job's three friends initially spent seven days sympathetically suffering with him in silence. After a week, they heaped accusations on him. They broke fellowship with Job. They did not stand with him. The fellowship was broken because his three friends drove a wedge of suspicion in their relationship. They essentially said, "Job, there must be something wrong with you."

These wedges were the work of Satan behind the scenes. Satan is not mentioned after Chapter 2 of Job, but his influence is throughout the book. Once Satan learned that Job's trust was not in possessions and health, Satan attacked Job through his relationships.

Pray, but carefully consider your prayers. Don't pray for God to change people because you don't know what people really need. Pray for wisdom to stand. Pray for the wisdom to unite. Pray for God to defend you.

Convince God that you really need Him. The difference between a victorious Christian and one who is a loser is that the former shows off his God while the latter tries to show off to God. People who are trying to prove that they can hold a relationship together are taking a whipping from Satan. Instead, you should show God that you need Him to hold the relationship together.

Chapter Thirteen

The Simple Solution

Most of my pastoral counseling addresses spiritual problems in families and marriages. They are relationships that have been divided just as Satan planned. The conflicts involve evil actions, revenge, divorce, and lawsuits. When the arguments are filled with angry, bitter, and sour words, the people have entered a spiritual battle. When the thoughts and posturing are negative, spiritual warfare has been declared and is being executed.

However, the spiritual problem was not the initial problem. Instead, the spiritual problem is the result of an initial problem. A person in need of counseling often says to me, "I never intended for it to go this far. This is not what I intended to happen when I started." Logic teaches that if we could avoid the initial problem, we would avoid the spiritual battles.

The best way to win in spiritual warfare is to completely avoid the battles. You will not lose if you do not have to battle. Psalm 119:133 says, *"Order my steps in thy word: and let not any iniquity have dominion over me."* The key to living a victorious Christian life is to have ordered steps. When iniquity has dominion over you, you are engaged in spiritual warfare. If your steps were ordered according to God's Word, you would circumvent many spiritual battles.

The first part of Psalm 119:133 is an intentionally practical statement: *"Order* [or organize] *my steps."* If you and God will plan your steps according to what God wrote in the Bible, then you will not have any spiritual iniquity dominating your life. People who have descended into spiritual warfare have failed to organize their steps according to God's Word.

Spiritual issues must be confronted with the Bible. The spiritual warfare that is waged from the lack of ordered steps can be corrected when one's steps are ordered according to the Bible. Confronting iniquity with truth creates great clashes and anger. Satan is going to resist the Word of God because he knows it will work.

Two reasons that God wrote the Bible were to tell us how He thinks and to tell us how He wants us to relate to Him. God understands that there is a great distance between you and Him in comprehension. *"For my thoughts are not your thoughts, neither are your ways my ways, saith the LORD."* (Isaiah 55:8) Since we cannot understand God completely and we cannot live up to His standards of perfection, He reaches us on our level.

God doesn't write us off because we don't achieve perfection. Instead, He offers us an example to follow. The Bible does not teach what God expects from us as much as it teaches how He operates. God likes order, plans, and procedures. He always keeps His Word. In essence, He obeys Himself.

Salvation exemplifies God's procedures. He will let anybody into Heaven who comes through Jesus Christ by way of the Cross. He always does that. There are no exceptions. God saves everybody who wants to get saved regardless of their age, race, or religion. His procedure for salvation is that a person confesses that Jesus is his Saviour.

If you are saved, you believe that God has a procedure for salvation. If God has a procedure for salvation, then He has procedures for other areas in life. God blesses laws and rules. An unsaved businessman will be more successful than a Christian businessman if he follows financial rules. God has procedures for how to maintain and cultivate your God-ordained relationships. God provides basic and core rules for life that order your steps and help circumvent spiritual warfare.

An Example From Marriage

A couple came for a counseling session because they were struggling in their marriage.

I asked, "What seems to be the problem?"

The wife quickly answered, "My husband seems to have another woman he likes." She started crying.

I asked the husband, "Do you have an affair going on?"

He replied, "Yes. I love this other woman."

I asked, "Do you love your wife also?"

"Well, I kind of love my wife, too, and I love this other woman. I am trying to decide between the two of them. I don't want to hurt my mistress by breaking up with her, and I don't want to hurt my wife by having an affair."

The couple had an incredible problem. The husband was torn between two women. As his pastor, I have to nurture this man so that he can accept God's ordered steps for his marriage. He didn't follow them. If he had followed them, he would not have his current spiritual warfare.

"You will have to choose one," I told him.

"I think I want my wife."

"Great. Then you have to let the mistress go."

"I don't want to let go of her."

"You have to follow some policy. You can't keep your wife and your girlfriend because neither will settle for you having both of them. Each of them wants you. You have to live by a rule. What rules do you live by in your marriage?"

The wife was hot under the collar. Her face was red. She was huffing and puffing. She felt rejected, angry, and neglected.

I changed my course of questioning. "Let's leave this mess and back up to when this started. Why did you start meeting this other woman?"

"My wife would nag and yell when I came home each night. I hated the strife between us. I don't have strife with this other woman."

"You've created a lot of strife."

"It was already there from her yelling. I found someone that I have peace with."

The wife said to him, "Let me tell you something. You never spend time with me. We never have a date. We never go out anywhere. You never spend any money on me. How much money have you spent on that girlfriend over there?"

"None of your business," he replied.

"It is my business. I am your wife. How much money do you spend on her? How many minutes do you spend on the phone with her? How much time do you spend with her? How come I don't get that time?"

They verbally sparred. It was spiritual warfare. There was tension. There was anger. There were words of regret spoken. As they argued, I asked God for wisdom. I opened my Bible to a passage on marriage. When they cooled down, I showed them a few verses of God's ordered steps for a marriage.

I said, "This battle that we are facing goes back to just bad planning in your marriage. When did you plan to spend time with your wife?"

He said, "I was busy, and I didn't have time to plan with her."

"But you make time to be with your girlfriend?"

"I call her every day."

I said, "You have a plan for your relationship with your girlfriend. Isn't it amazing that you plan to talk to your girlfriend, and your relationship with her is soaring so well that you want to keep it? Doesn't it make sense that your relationship with your wife is dying because it is neglected and unplanned? Do you think there is any correlation there?"

The policy for my marriage is that there is only one woman and I've already found her. "I want to be happy" is the policy that most people live by. My policy eliminates Internet chat rooms with unknown women, girlfriends on the side, entertaining other women in my mind, and pornography. I do not fight the spiritual battle of unplanned behavior because I order my steps in the Bible. Some might say that my behavior is extreme, but I'd say that I have a great marriage, and I don't need to seek marriage advice from others. I have no women that I need to shut up. I have no secrets that I fear will be discovered.

An Example From a Pastor

I travel and speak in churches approximately every other week. I spend much time during those days meeting with pastors from the local areas. At a certain meeting one pastor asked, "Can I have just a few minutes of your time in private?"

I said, "Yes."

He asked, "In a real quick nutshell, what is the secret to First Baptist Church's success?"

I said, "It is work. How are you doing with that?"

"Will you elaborate on that?" he asked.

I replied, "How many hours do you put in each week? I don'
mean sitting in your office doing nothing and reading magazines.
mean working hours."

"I probably put in about 40 to 45 hours," he answered.

"I put in 85. How is your church doing?"

He said, "It's struggling."

I said, "Okay, why don't you plan to work? It might surprise yo
If you put in as many hours as Donald Trump does, you might s
Donald Trump's success. If you put in as many hours as Bill Gat
puts in, you might see Bill Gates' success. If you apply yourself
the rules and policies that Jack Hyles used in building a churc
you might see Jack Hyles' success. Everyone wants to know wh
will bring God's hand of blessing. God blesses the people wh
follow a plan, a law, a rule, or a principle."

An Example From George Washington

God wrote a book of policies by which to live. Godliness w
be achieved if you will set policies and live by them. Isn't th
what George Washington did? When he was a teenager, he wrot
whole list of the virtues and matters of integrity by which he live
George Washington decided at an early age how he would condu
his business, how he would respect his elders, how he watched
tongue, and how he responded to criticism. I'm not surprised th
he was a founding father of our nation. I am not surprised that
left Valley Forge with a ragtag army of soldiers that were freezi
to death and beat the trained, professional British army. I'm n
surprised that we have monuments and streets and cities nam
after him. He was blessed because he followed procedures.

Reflecting on Your Position

What rules govern your life? By what policies do you live? How many books have you read that will help you establish policies for your life? What rules do you have for rearing your children? What rules do you follow for spanking your children? What rules do you have to keep your marriage pure? What procedures govern your finances? Are you poisoning your life with procedures that are not acceptable to God?

Advice for the Christian Engaged in Spiritual Warfare

Plan your life instead of living a reactionary life. Wake up at a set time instead of when you feel like waking up. Plan to eat good foods instead of eating at whim. Most people eat when they feel like eating and disregard whether or not it is healthy food.

Waking up is just one example, but you feel better when you follow a plan. When I sleep in for an extra 30 to 90 minutes, I feel crummy even though I strongly felt that I needed sleep. People who sleep in might put off their Bible reading, breakfast, or needed grooming. The lack of routine makes people irritated and agitated throughout the day.

The Christian life is a life of discipline and hard work. Salvation doesn't take your problems away; it takes you to Heaven someday. A saved person must work hard to keep his spouse happy, rear his kids, and keep his finances in order.

A planned life helps you to recover from setbacks because you know what road you were on. People with no plan lose their direction. A plan is like a compass that keeps you on the path. Live a life that is on purpose.

Establish the policies for your life. Twenty years ago I discovered that salads do not agree with my digestive system. I went to the doctor after suffering for several years, and he told me that I have a disease that resembles Crohn's disease. He advised me to avoid the foods that incite the disease. Because of his advice, I haven't eaten a salad in 20 years. I would love to have one, but for the sake of my health, I have a rule to avoid salad.

The Bible doesn't say, "Thou shalt not eat lettuce!" I have instituted a rule in my life because it protects me. The Bible doesn't say, "Thou shalt not ride in a car alone with another woman!" But I don't ride in a car alone with other women because it keeps my marriage far from the cliff of infidelity.

Let policies rule your life. When you follow policies, you avoid conflict. If you avoid conflict, you avoid verbal arguments which result in spiritual warfare.

The basic areas where you should establish a plan are in your walk with God, marriage, child rearing, dating, and finances. Read books on these topics that will help you establish plans. Sit down with your spouse and discuss rules that you will implement in your home. My wife and I established a list of reasons we would spank our children. The list was posted on the refrigerator for the kids to see. We never deviated from the list because it was our policy.

Don't miss the simplicity of this lesson. There is not a cute formula for winning in spiritual warfare. Many of your problems are the consequence of an unplanned life. Let your life be guided by policies based on the Word of God.

The business of the Christian life is not learning how to fight the devil. The business of the Christian life is learning how to live a disciplined life so that your life is protected by the power of God and filled with grace. The presence of God will empower your life when you order your steps in the Word of God. The presence of God will defeat Satan's attacks in spiritual warfare.